WALKING
NEW YORK

WALKING

NEW YORK

THE BEST OF THE CITY

Katherine Cancila

NATIONAL GEOGRAPHIC

Washington, D.C.

WALKING
NEW YORK

CONTENTS

6 INTRODUCTION
8 VISITING NEW YORK
10 USING THIS GUIDE

PART 1

PAGE 12
WHIRLWIND TOURS

14 NEW YORK IN A DAY
18 NEW YORK IN A WEEKEND
24 NEW YORK FOR FUN
28 NEW YORK IN A WEEKEND WITH KIDS

PART 2

PAGE 36
NEW YORK'S NEIGHBORHOODS

40 LOWER MANHATTAN
56 THE VILLAGES
70 MIDTOWN SOUTH
86 MIDTOWN NORTH
102 UPPER EAST SIDE
120 CENTRAL PARK
132 UPPER WEST SIDE
146 THE HEIGHTS & HARLEM
158 BROOKLYN

PART 3

PAGE 174
TRAVEL ESSENTIALS

176 TRAVEL ESSENTIALS
180 HOTELS

188 INDEX
191 CREDITS

Previous pages: Washington Square Park; left: Manhattan Bridge; right: doll from the Museum of the City of New York; above right: the Metropolitan Museum of Art; bottom right: Brooklyn Heights Promenade

Introduction

The first time I walked New York was with my uncle Buck. I was about six. He lived in Stuyvesant Town—known as Stuy Town and named for Peter Stuyvesant, the last director general of the Dutch colony of New Amsterdam. I remember the challenge of striding down the sidewalk, navigating the endless surge of humanity that came toward me. Later, I lived a stone's throw from Stuy Town, across from Tompkins Square Park. I spent hours on summer Saturdays sitting in the park, a tourist in my own neighborhood.

New York is the sum of its neighborhoods and the expression of endless waves of usually temporary citizens who come to make their mark and then move on. It is a city of and for walkers. Gawk at the ground-to-sky buildings—they seem more imposing and stylish here than in any other great world city. Snack at a corner street cart or sit in one of New York's hundreds of parks.

New York on a summer's day: Behind Central Park rise some of the art deco buildings that distinguish midtown Manhattan.

Make this book your companion. It celebrates the art of the New York walk, and abundantly delivers the how and where of doing it well. Want to do a whirlwind tour in a day? We have it. With kids? That, too. And, most important, we recognize what is becoming true of cities everywhere. You don't really visit a city; you visit its neighborhoods. This guide is engineered with that in mind—the key to a place whose bustling core measures just 34 square miles (88 sq km) and probably has more must-sees than any other city on the planet.

Keith Bellows

Editor in Chief, National Geographic Traveler *magazine*

Visiting New York

Few cities rival New York for cultural diversity, vibrant street life, world-class art and music, and sheer excitement. Much of this energy is packed into a narrow island just over 13 miles (21 km) long, so finding your feet can be a challenge.

New York Neighborhoods

It makes sense to approach Manhattan neighborhood by neighborhood, since each has a special character and attractions. If history is your thing, head for the southern tip of Manhattan to get a feeling of the city's preeminence as a trading port, then as a destination for European immigrants. Savor its literary past by strolling the tranquil streets of Greenwich Village, or track down the alternative spirit still alive in the East Village. Art lovers should zero in on the museums of the Upper East Side, and head up to Harlem for Latino culture and a dip into glorious medieval art at The Cloisters. For visitors with more time, Brooklyn's superb museums, Prospect Park, and Botanical Garden beckon, along with great eateries.

New York Day-by-Day

Open every day (with some exceptions for major holidays) American Museum of Natural History, Central Park Zoo, Empire State Building, The Lower East Side Tenement Museum, Madame Tussauds, National Museum of the Native American, The New York City Police Museum, Rockefeller Center, St. Patrick's Cathedral, Statue of Liberty and Ellis Island.

Monday Most museums are closed except for above and the Merchant's House Museum, Museum of Modern Art (MoMA), Solomon R. Guggenheim Museum, and The Jewish Museum.

Tuesday Brooklyn Museum, Merchant's House Museum, MoMA, Morris-Jumel Mansion, Studio Museum, Harlem, and Whitney Museum of American Art are closed.

Wednesday The Jewish Museum, Merchant's House Museum, and Studio Museum, Harlem are closed.

Thursday The Guggenheim Museum is closed. The National Museum of the Native American is open until 9 p.m.

Friday The Metropolitan Museum of Art (Met) is open until 9 p.m., MoMA until 8 p.m.

Saturday The Met is open until 9 p.m.; the Jewish Museum is free.

Sunday The New York Public Library is closed.

The quiet streets of Greenwich Village break with the grid pattern of the rest of Manhattan and offer a wide range of independent shops and restaurants.

Taking a Break

Walking can get tiring, so note the places on your route where you can take a break. There are tiny parks and green spaces just off some main drags, and big public areas such as Rockefeller Plaza and the David Rubenstein Atrium at Lincoln Center. Or hop on a bus to get a rest while seeing the sights.

Enjoying New York for Less

Sometimes, depending on the season, there are free performances on offer. At Lincoln Center's David Rubenstein Atrium, for example, concerts of all kinds are presented every Thursday evening. Drop by its information hub to find out about these, and about free recitals by students from the Juilliard School. In June and July "Shakespeare in the Park" plays at the Delacorte Theater in Central Park. Tickets are free online or beginning at 1 p.m. at the theater (www.shakespeareinthepark .org). Most Broadway theaters also sell discounted standing-room-only tickets just before a show. Some museums have free entry at certain times, such as MoMA on Friday evenings. For visiting six of the major attractions, a City Pass (www.citypass.com/new-york) saves both money and time waiting in line.

Using This Guide

Each tour—which might be only a walk, or might take advantage of the city's
public transportation as well—is plotted on a map and has been planned to take
into account opening hours and the times of day when sites are less crowded.
Many end near restaurants, theaters, or lively night spots for evening activities.

Whirlwind Tours

Whirlwind Tours are for people
who have only a day or a
weekend to spend in the city and
want to be sure that they see the
best of the best. Choose your
tour based on your time and
interests: One Day; Weekend
(Day 1 & Day 2); For Fun; and
With Kids (Day 1 & Day 2).

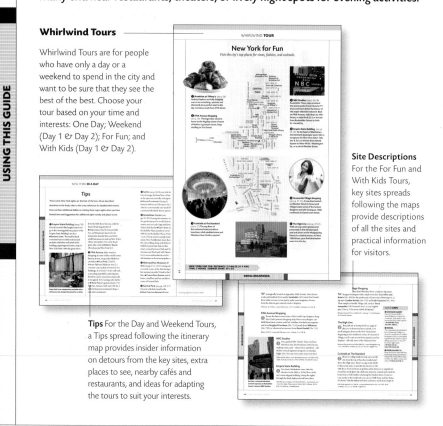

Site Descriptions
For the For Fun and
With Kids Tours,
key sites spreads
following the maps
provide descriptions
of all the sites and
practical information
for visitors.

Tips For the Day and Weekend Tours,
a Tips spread following the itinerary
map provides insider information
on detours from the key sites, extra
places to see, nearby cafés and
restaurants, and ideas for adapting
the tours to suit your interests.

Neighborhood Tours

The nine neighborhood tours each begin with an introduction, followed by an itinerary map highlighting the key sites that make up the tour and detailed key sites descriptions. Each tour is followed by an "in-depth" spread showcasing one major site along the route, a "distinctly" New York spread providing background information on a quintessential element of that neighborhood, and a "best of" spread that groups sites thematically.

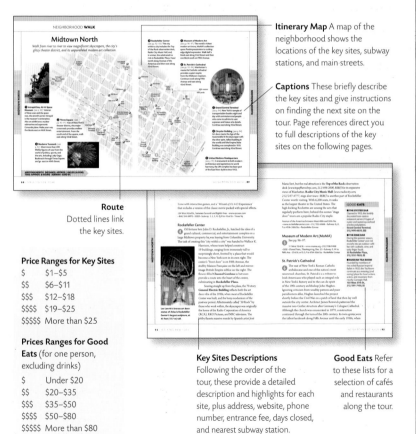

Itinerary Map A map of the neighborhood shows the locations of the key sites, subway stations, and main streets.

Captions These briefly describe the key sites and give instructions on finding the next site on the tour. Page references direct you to full descriptions of the key sites on the following pages.

Route Dotted lines link the key sites.

Price Ranges for Key Sites

$	$1–$5
$$	$6–$11
$$$	$12–$18
$$$$	$19–$25
$$$$$	More than $25

Prices Ranges for Good Eats (for one person, excluding drinks)

$	Under $20
$$	$20–$35
$$$	$35–$50
$$$$	$50–$80
$$$$$	More than $80

Key Sites Descriptions Following the order of the tour, these provide a detailed description and highlights for each site, plus address, website, phone number, entrance fee, days closed, and nearest subway station.

Good Eats Refer to these lists for a selection of cafés and restaurants along the tour.

PART 1

Whirlwind Tours

New York in a Day

Visit the tallest building, shop in a favorite store, stroll in the city's greenest space, and join the Times Square party.

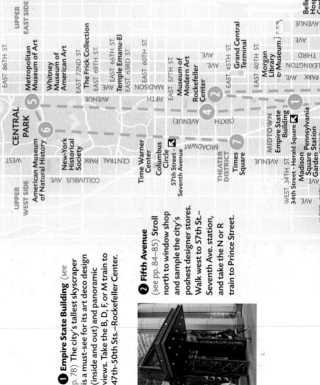

❶ Empire State Building (see p. 78) The city's tallest skyscraper is a must-see for its art deco design (inside and out) and panoramic views. Take the B, D, F, or M train to 47th–50th Sts.–Rockefeller Center.

❷ Fifth Avenue (see pp. 84–85) Stroll north to window shop and sample the city's poshest designer stores. Walk west to 57th St.–Seventh Ave. station, and take the N or R train to Prince Street.

❹ Rockefeller Center (see pp. 92–93) The home of NBC studios and Radio City Music Hall also boasts the Top of the Rock observation deck. After feasting on the views, take a cab uptown.

❺ Metropolitan Museum of Art (see pp. 112–115) The largest museum in the western hemisphere has more than two million works of art spanning 5,000 years. Walk west to Central Park.

❻ Central Park (see pp. 120–127) Among the park's many highlights is Belvedere Castle, a large stone structure built in 1869 that promises excellent views of the park and likely bird sightings. Exit the park on Fifth Avenue and take a cab to 42nd Street in Times Square.

UPPER WEST SIDE

UPPER EAST SIDE

American Museum of Natural History

New-York Historical Society

CENTRAL PARK ❻

Metropolitan Museum of Art ❺

Whitney Museum of American Art

EAST 86TH ST.

EAST 72ND ST.

The Frick Collection

EAST 69TH ST.

EAST 66TH ST.

Temple Emanu-El

EAST 63RD ST.

EAST 60TH ST.

Time Warner Center

Columbus Circle

57th Street - Seventh Avenue

EAST 57TH ST.

Museum of Modern Art ❹

Rockefeller Center

EAST 45TH ST.

Grand Central Terminal

Morgan Library & Museum

EAST 40TH ST.

THEATER DISTRICT

Times Square ❼

MIDTOWN

Empire State Building ❶

WEST 34TH ST. - Herald Square

34th Street - Herald Square

Madison Square Pennsylvania Garden Station

WEST 28TH

COLUMBUS AVE.

CENTRAL PARK WEST

BROADWAY

AVENUE (SEVENTH AVENUE)

AVENUE (SIXTH AVENUE)

FIFTH AVENUE

MADISON AVENUE

PARK AVE.

LEXINGTON AVE.

THIRD AVENUE

Bellevue Hospital Center

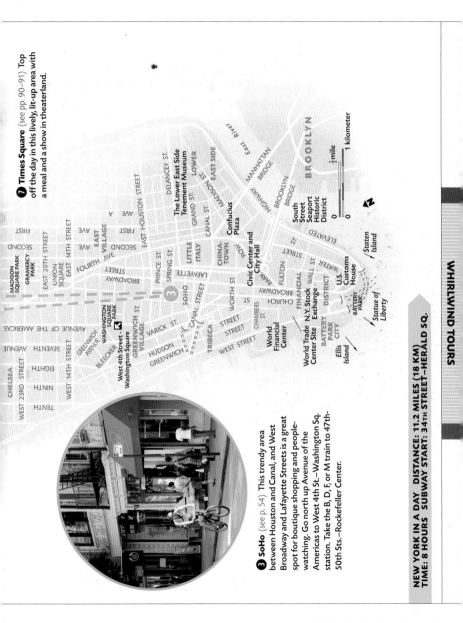

⑦ Times Square (see pp. 90–91) Top off the day in this lively, lit-up area with a meal and a show in theaterland.

③ SoHo (see p. 54) This trendy area between Houston and Canal, and West Broadway and Lafayette Streets is a great spot for boutique shopping and people-watching. Go north up Avenue of the Americas to West 4th St. – Washington Sq. station. Take the B, D, F, or M train to 47th–50th Sts.–Rockefeller Center.

The Lower East Side Tenement Museum

Confucius Plaza

LOWER EAST SIDE

EAST VILLAGE

LITTLE ITALY

CHINA-TOWN

Civic Center and City Hall

FINANCIAL DISTRICT

N.Y. Stock Exchange

U.S. Customs House

World Trade Center Site

World Financial Center

BATTERY PARK CITY

TRIBECA

SOHO

GREENWICH VILLAGE

WASHINGTON SQUARE PARK

West 4th Street – Washington Square

CHELSEA

EAST VILLAGE

GRAMERCY PARK

MADISON SQUARE PARK

UNION SQUARE

South Street Seaport Historic District

MANHATTAN BRIDGE

BROOKLYN BRIDGE

BROOKLYN

Statue of Liberty

Ellis Island

Staten Island

East River

N

0   ½ mile
0   1 kilometer

NEW YORK IN A DAY   DISTANCE: 11.2 MILES (18 KM)
TIME: 8 HOURS   SUBWAY START: 34TH STREET–HERALD SQ.

Tips

These iconic New York sights are the best of the best. All are described elsewhere in the book; refer to the cross-references for detailed information. Here you have additional tidbits on visiting these major sights when you have limited time and suggestions for additional sights nearby and places to eat.

❶ Empire State Building (see p. 78)
Even if you don't like heights and won't go to the viewing platform, pop in to the Empire State Building's art deco ■ ENTRANCE LOBBY. The marble-lined room has been recently restored and includes a fabulous wall relief of the building, superimposed onto a map of New York State. After the great views from the 86th-floor balcony, walk the dense, block-long stretch of ■ KOREATOWN (*32nd St. between Fifth Ave. and Broadway*), known for its restaurants, karaoke bars, and other small businesses, to soak up New York's ethnic atmosphere. For some shady quiet, take a rest in ■ GREELEY SQUARE (*Broadway and West 32nd St.*).

❷ Fifth Avenue After window shopping at some of the world's most famous stores, escape the Midtown crowds in ■ PALEY PARK (*53rd St. between Fifth and Madison Aves.*), a concrete oasis tucked in between two buildings. A 25-foot (7.6 m) wall with a cascading waterfall, scattered patio furniture, and a concession stand add to its appeal. If it's raining, take shelter in ■ TRUMP TOWER's grand atrium (*725 Fifth Ave., between 56th and 57th Sts.*), with its luxurious menswear shop, a café, and a restaurant.

Paley Park is an unexpected, secluded niche where you can escape the street for a while.

WHIRLWIND TOURS

❸ SoHo (see p. 54) If your kids have lots of energy, let them blow off steam in the spacious, recently redesigned ■ VESUVIO PLAYGROUND (*Spring St. between Sullivan and Thompson Sts.*), which is conveniently surrounded by casual and affordable lunch options.

❹ Rockefeller Center (see pp. 92–93) During the summer, catch free performances by world-famous artists, such as Lady Gaga and James Taylor, held by the ■ TODAY SHOW at Rockefeller Plaza (*southwest corner of 49th St. and Rockefeller Plaza, Friday 7 a.m.*). If you want to sample some classic New York ■ STREET FOOD, then try the carts selling cheap and delicious Middle Eastern fare that dot the street corners between Park and Sixth Avenues and 42nd and 56th Streets. Go to *www.midtownlunch.com* for information on the most popular carts.

❺ Metropolitan Museum of Art (see pp. 112–115) Craving a less crowded corner of the Met during the hot summer months? Head to the fifth floor ■ CANTOR ROOF GARDEN, which hosts a small bar and has excellent views of Central Park.

❻ Central Park (see pp. 120–127) If you're with kids, head to the ■ HANS CHRISTIAN ANDERSEN STATUE

CUSTOMIZING **YOUR DAY**

In spring and summer months, when it stays light until early evening, it's best to visit the Met before Central Park in order to see as much as possible before closing time. In the fall and winter, however, it becomes dark and cold far earlier, so be sure to get to Central Park by 3 p.m. in order to see the park in daylight and the Met before it closes.

(*by Conservatory Water*) where, on Saturday afternoons during summer, there are readings of Hans Andersen's much loved stories. Birdwatchers should visit ■ THE RAMBLE (*mid-park by 79th St.*), a 37-acre (15 ha) wood, home to more than 250 bird species.

❼ Times Square (see pp. 90–91) Commune with the ghosts of writers while sipping a delicious pre-dinner drink at the storied literary haunt, ■ THE ALGONQUIN hotel (*59 West 44th St., between Fifth and Sixth Aves.*). As you cross Times Square, look for the old *New York Times* building's famous ■ TICKERTAPE to catch up on the day's news. For dinner, check out ■ SARDI'S (*234 West 44th St., 212/221-8440, $$$$*), which offers a lively dining experience within caricature-covered walls, with a signature dish of steak tartare prepared at your table.

WHIRLWIND TOURS

New York in a Weekend

DAY 1

Midtown & Central Park

Intersperse the most popular sites with moments of peace and quiet.

❹ **Museum of Modern Art** (see pp. 96–97) Among the world's most significant collections of modern art, the recently renovated MoMA houses Vincent van Gogh's "The Starry Night" and Andy Warhol's "Campbell's Soup Cans." Retrace your steps and continue north on Fifth Avenue.

❸ **St. Patrick's Cathedral** (see pp. 93–94) One of the country's largest and most famous Catholic cathedrals, St. Patrick's offers a break from the Midtown landscape and the chance of a quiet moment. Continue north on Fifth Avenue to 53rd Street and turn west.

❷ **Rockefeller Center** (see pp. 92–93) Landmark art deco buildings and sculptures, along with nearly 150 places to shop and eat make this complex a top destination for locals and tourists alike. Walk east on 49th Street to Fifth Avenue and head north.

❺ **Central Park** (see pp. 120–127) Push past the horse-drawn carriages and make a beeline for the wide, tree-lined walkway known as The Mall, which starts mid-park at 66th Street. When you leave the park, take a cab downtown to 42nd Street in Times Square.

Map labels:
COLUMBUS
New-York Historical Society
American Museum of Natural History
Lincoln Center for the Performing Arts
Time Warner Center
Columbus Circle
CENTRAL PARK
Metropolitan Museum of Art
EAST 76TH STREET
Whitney Museum of American Art
EAST 72ND ST.
The Frick Collection
EAST 69TH ST.
EAST 66TH ST.
Temple Emanu-El
EAST 63RD ST.
EAST 60TH ST.
EAST 57TH ST.
Museum of Modern Art
St. Patrick's Cathedral
Rockefeller Center
Grand Central Terminal
New York Public Library
WEST 57TH STREET
WEST 54TH STREET
WEST 51ST STREET
WEST 48TH STREET
WEST 42ND ST.
CENTRAL PARK WEST
BROADWAY
SIXTH AVENUE
THEATER DISTRICT
Times Square

1 Empire State Building (see p. 78) This 1,250-foot (381 m) skyscraper has been captured in such classic films as *King Kong* and *An Affair to Remember*. Walk north on Fifth Avenue and west on 34th Street. Take the B, D, F, or M train at 34th St.–Herald Sq. station to 47th–50th Sts.–Rockefeller Center.

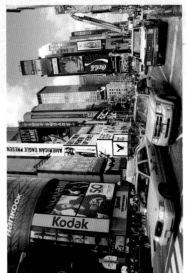

Jacob Javits Convention Center
MIDTOWN
Empire State Building
Morgan Library & Museum
WEST 34TH STREET · EAST 34TH STREET
34th Street–Herald Square
Madison Square Garden · Pennsylvania Station
SECOND
WEST 28TH STREET
CHELSEA
THIRD
LEXINGTON
WEST 23RD STREET
MADISON AVENUE
PARK AVE
MADISON SQUARE PARK
EAST 23RD ST.
WEST 14TH STREET
AVENUE OF THE AMERICAS
FIFTH
GRAMERCY PARK
EAST 20TH ST.
GREENWICH AVENUE
SEVENTH AVENUE
EIGHTH AVENUE
UNION SQUARE
NINTH AVENUE
TENTH
ELEVENTH AVE

0   ½ mile
0   1 kilometer

6 Times Square (see pp. 90–91) Once tawdry and unsafe, this bustling, neon-lit area is now among the city's most tourist-friendly spots. Walk to your chosen Broadway theater, whether your taste is for blockbuster musical or edgy drama.

NEW YORK IN A WEEKEND   DISTANCE: 4 MILES (6.4 KM)
TIME: 8 HOURS   SUBWAY START: 34TH STREET–HERALD SQ.

New York in a Weekend

Downtown

Classic sights combine with high fashion.

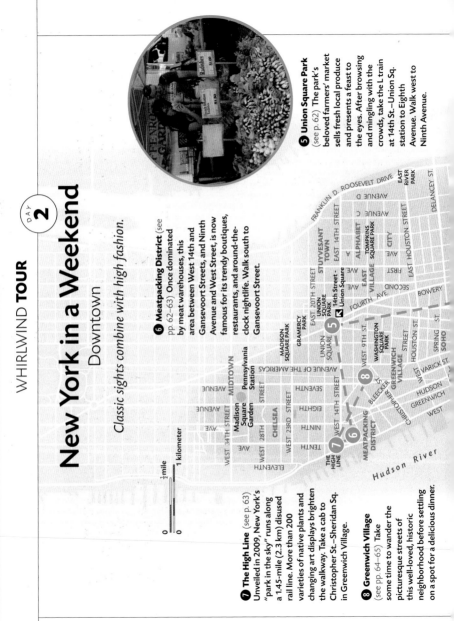

6 Meatpacking District (see pp. 62–63) Once dominated by meat warehouses, this area between West 14th and Gansevoort Streets, and Ninth Avenue and West Street, is now famous for its trendy boutiques, restaurants, and around-the-clock nightlife. Walk south to Gansevoort Street.

5 Union Square Park (see p. 62) The park's beloved farmers' market sells fresh local produce and presents a feast to the eyes. After browsing and mingling with the crowds, take the L train at 14th St.–Union Sq. station to Eighth Avenue. Walk west to Ninth Avenue.

7 The High Line (see p. 63) Unveiled in 2009, New York's "park in the sky" runs along a 1.45-mile (2.3 km) disused rail line. More than 200 varieties of native plants and changing art displays brighten the walkway. Take a cab to Christopher St.–Sheridan Sq. in Greenwich Village.

8 Greenwich Village (see pp. 64–65) Take some time to wander the picturesque streets of this well-loved, historic neighborhood before settling on a spot for a delicious dinner.

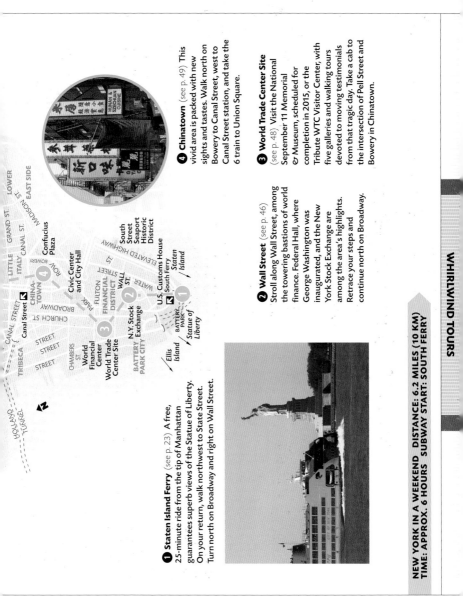

① Staten Island Ferry (see p. 23) A free, 25-minute ride from the tip of Manhattan guarantees superb views of the Statue of Liberty. On your return, walk northwest to State Street. Turn north on Broadway and right on Wall Street.

② Wall Street (see p. 46) Stroll along Wall Street, among the towering bastions of world finance. Federal Hall, where George Washington was inaugurated, and the New York Stock Exchange are among the area's highlights. Retrace your steps and continue north on Broadway.

③ World Trade Center Site (see p. 48) Visit the National September 11 Memorial & Museum, scheduled for completion in 2015, or the Tribute WTC Visitor Center, with five galleries and walking tours devoted to moving testimonials from that tragic day. Take a cab to the intersection of Pell Street and Bowery in Chinatown.

④ Chinatown (see p. 49) This vivid area is packed with new sights and tastes. Walk north on Bowery to Canal Street, west to Canal Street station, and take the 6 train to Union Square.

NEW YORK IN A WEEKEND   DISTANCE: 6.2 MILES (10 KM)
TIME: APPROX. 6 HOURS   SUBWAY START: SOUTH FERRY

Tips

These major New York sights can be seen in two days. Refer to the cross-references for detailed information elsewhere in the book. Here you'll find information on detours to nearby sights and local cafés and restaurants and suggestions for customizing the tour to suit your own interests.

DAY 1

❷ **Rockefeller Center** (see pp. 92–93) Before or after, detour one block south to ■ **DIAMOND ROW** (*47th St. between 5th and 6th Aves.*), a world of priceless gems.

❸ **St. Patrick's Cathedral** (see pp. 93–94) Before you go, check out the busy program of ■ **FREE CONCERTS** of

MoMA's The Modern offers French-American cuisine and more than 900 wine selections.

choir or organ music, and the service schedule. Mass is held several times a day; some are music masses and the 4 p.m. Sunday service is in Spanish.

❹ **Museum of Modern Art** (see pp. 96–97) Combine your visit with fine dining and book in advance for ■ **THE MODERN,** run by the celebrated restaurateur Danny Meyer, who also runs the two museum cafés.
■ **CAFE 2** on the second floor serves panini, pasta, and salads, and has an espresso bar. ■ **TERRACE 5** on the fifth floor notches up the sophistication level with wine-tasting and artisanal cheeses. It has views of the central Sculpture Garden and the skyline, and you can dine on the terrace seasonally.

❺ **Central Park** (see pp. 120–127) Before your visit, make a quick detour to check out the free exhibitions at ■ **THE GROLIER CLUB** (*47 East 60th St.,* between Madison and Park Aves.), the country's oldest society for lovers of books and the graphic arts.

DAY 2

❶ Staten Island Ferry (*Whitehall Terminal, 1 South St., www.siferry.com, Subway: 1, R, W to South Ferry*) Don't forget a ■ JACKET, as the winds can be chilly, even in summertime. You have to ■ DEBARK ON ARRIVAL at the island and reboard via the waiting room.

❷ Wall Street (*see pp. 46–47*) While you're in the vicinity, take a rest from the intensely financial milieu and savor the spiritual feel of the Gothic Revival-style ■ TRINITY CHURCH (*see pp. 47–48*).

❹ Chinatown (*see p. 49*) The city's oldest spot for dim sum is ■ NOM WAH TEA PARLOR (*13 Doyers St., near Bowery*), which—refreshingly—hasn't changed much since it opened in 1920. At ■ FOOD SING 88 (*2 East Broadway, between Chatham Sq. and St. James Pl.*), you can watch noodles stretched, swung, and folded, then enjoy them in a bowl of soup. For a restful break after walking through Chinatown, visit the ■ LIZ CHRISTY BOWERY-HOUSTON GARDEN (*corner of Houston St. and Bowery*), the city's first community garden.

CUSTOMIZING **YOUR DAY**

If modern art is not for you, other art options beckon a short $10-15 cab ride away from St. Patrick's Cathedral. The enormous **Metropolitan Museum of Art** (see pp. 112–115) is truly comprehensive. **The Frick Collection** (see p. 106), housed in the former residence of industrialist and art collector Henry Clay Frick, is a smaller, more intimate choice, and even closer.

❼ The High Line (*see p. 63*) Don't miss the amphitheater-like ■ 10TH AVENUE SQUARE, above the 10th Avenue–17th Street crossing, with its views of Midtown and the Statue of Liberty.

❽ Greenwich Village (*see pp. 64–65*) Among the great dining options in the Village is ■ BLUE RIBBON BAKERY KITCHEN (*35 Downing St.*), lined with windows upstairs, and cozy and cavernous downstairs. Freshly baked bread is brought to your table from the refurbished 19th-century oven. It is part of an empire of fun, late-night spots, with terrific but casual service and big, delicious portions. Or try ■ PEARL OYSTER BAR (*18 Cornelia St.*), always packed and lively. The seafood is super-fresh, with lobster rolls and shoestring fries one of the best dishes on the menu.

New York for Fun

Visit the city's top places for views, fashion, and cocktails.

❶ Breakfast at Tiffany's (see p. 26)
Audrey Hepburn as Holly Golightly
was on to something—pastries and
diamonds are a perfect start to the
day. Continue south from 57th Street.

❷ Fifth Avenue Shopping
(see p. 26) This legendary street is
home to the flagship stores of some
of fashion's greatest names. Keep
strolling to 51st Street.

❸ NBC Studios (see p. 26) At
Rockefeller Plaza, enjoy a behind-
the-scenes peek of your favorite TV
show and learn about the history of
this major television network. Back
on Fifth Avenue, walk down to 34th
Street, or take the B, D, F, or M train
from Rockefeller Center to 34th
St.–Herald Sq.

❹ Empire State Building (see pp.
26, 78) At the heart of Manhattan,
the landmark skyscraper never fails to
enrapture the first-time visitor. Take
the B, D, F, or M train from Herald
Square to West 4th St.–Washington
Sq., or a cab to Bleecker Street.

Metropolitan
Museum of Art

Whitney
Museum of
American Art

The Frick Collection

EAST 72ND ST.

EAST 69TH ST.

EAST 66TH ST.

EAST 63RD ST.

CENTRAL
PARK

Temple
Emanu-El

EAST 60TH ST.

Breakfast
at Tiffany's

❶

Museum of
Modern Art

EAST 57TH ST.

SECOND

Time Warner
Center

Columbus
Circle

CENTRAL PARK
SOUTH

57th Street

NBC
Studios

❸

AVE

AVE

EAST 45TH ST.

Grand
Central
Terminal

AVE

New York Public Library

MIDTOWN

Morgan Library
& Museum

EAST 34TH ST.

THIRD

LEXINGTON

PARK

MADISON

FIFTH

CENTRAL PARK WEST

BROADWAY

SIXTH AVENUE

AVENUE

AVENUE

THEATER
DISTRICT

Times
Square

WEST 42ND ST.

AVENUE

AVE

Empire State
Building

❹

34th Street – Herald Square

Pennsylvania
Station

STREET

LINCOLN TUNNEL

Jacob Javits
Convention Center

WEST 34TH STREET

Madison
Square Garden

WEST 28TH

AVE

AVENUE

0 ½ mile

0 1 kilometer

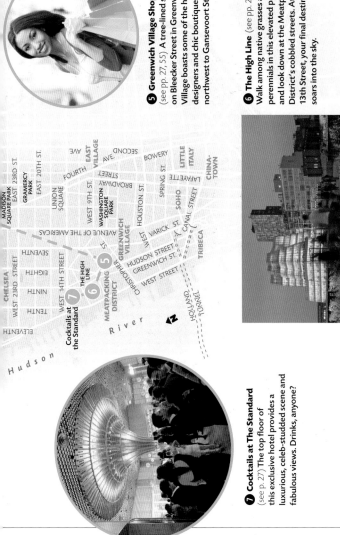

5 Greenwich Village Shopping
(see pp. 27, 55) A tree-lined stretch on Bleecker Street in Greenwich Village boasts some of the hottest designers and chic boutiques. Walk northwest to Gansevoort Street.

6 The High Line (see pp. 27, 63) Walk among native grasses and perennials in this elevated park and look down at the Meatpacking District's cobbled streets. At West 13th Street, your final destination soars into the sky.

7 Cocktails at The Standard (see p. 27) The top floor of this exclusive hotel provides a luxurious, celeb-studded scene and fabulous views. Drinks, anyone?

NEW YORK FOR FUN DISTANCE: 7.3 MILES (11.7 KM)
TIME: 7 HOURS SUBWAY START: 57TH ST.

Breakfast at Tiffany's

1 Start at the most dreamy of luxury stores: Tiffany & Co., strategically located on legendary Fifth Avenue. First choose a takeout breakfast from nearby **Sarabeth's** (*40 Central Park South*), then while you savor your pastry, make your imaginary choices from the famous gem-starred window displays.

Fifth Ave. at 57th St. • www.tiffany.com • 212/755-8000 • Subway: F to 57th St.

Fifth Avenue Shopping

2 Peruse the latest concoctions of the world's top designers along New York's premier shopping strip. Here every shopper can fulfill their haute couture wish list, whether it includes an exquisite suit from **Bergdorf Goodman** (*No. 754*), pearls from **Mikimoto** (*No. 730*), or whimsical accessories from **Henri Bendel** (*No. 712*).

Below 57th St. • www.visit5thavenue.com • Subway: F to 57th St.

See how a national television network operates at Rockefeller Center's historic NBC Studios.

NBC Studios

3 On a guided NBC Studio Tour, you'll see television sets, the broadcast control room, makeup room, and—when not in operation—the studios of such signature programs as Saturday Night Live. You can even create your own show.

30 Rockefeller Plaza • www.nbcstudiotour.com • 212/664-3700 • $$$$ • Subway: F, D, B, V to 47th-50th Sts.–Rockefeller Center

Empire State Building

4 For classic Manhattan views, take the elevator to the 86th or 102nd floor of the city's most elegant building. Sweep the sights through the fixed, high-powered binoculars.

350 Fifth Ave., between 33rd and 34th Sts. • www.esbnyc.com • 212/736-3100 • Observatory tickets: $$$$ • Subway: B, D, F, N,Q, R to 34th St.–Herald Square

Greenwich Village Shopping

5 Downtown, tree-lined Bleecker Street combines big-name designer boutiques with a small town feel. Shop **Olive and Bette's** *(No. 384)* for the perfect pair of jeans and a flattering tee, or dip into **Cynthia Rowley** *(No. 376)* and **Lulu Guinness** *(No. 394)*. Then sample a friendly Village café, such as **Tea & Sympathy** *(108 Greenwich Ave.)*, a cozy English gem. (See p. 55 for more stylish shopping.)

Between Seventh Ave. and Bank St. • Subway: 1 to Christopher St.–Sheridan Square

The High Line

6 This park set at treetop level is a magical place to sit down and sun yourself, or to stroll and gaze down on the New York streets. Beginning in the northwest corner of Greenwich Village, you'll come across flower patches and art displays—all with views of the Hudson River.

Between Gansevoort and West 30th Sts. • www.thehighline.org • 212/500-6035 • Subway: A,C, E, L to 14th St.–Eighth Ave.

Cocktails at The Standard

7 Floor-to-ceiling windows look out over the city from the top of this uber-trendy hotel above the High Line. There's no sign in the lobby to this secret aerie, so just take the elevator to the 18th floor. From hostesses in goddess-style dresses to a magnificent round bar, it's all glam. Sip a delicious, if pricey, cocktail and watch the boats from a white leather sofa facing the Hudson River. From two cozy nooks on the south side, you can see Wall Street and the Statue of Liberty. Visit the bathroom before you leave; you'll never forget it!

848 Washington St. at 13th St.• www.standardhotels.com • 212/645-4646 • Subway: A, C, E, L to 14th St.–Eighth Ave.

GOOD **EATS**

■ **BOUCHON BAKERY**
Pop into Thomas Keller's second Midtown outpost for a croissant, fresh salad, or the renowned chef's classic quiche. **1 Rockefeller Plaza, 212/782-3890, $**

■ **FEDORA**
This renovated and relaunched bar in Greenwich Village is a must for cocktail lovers. Leather banquettes, fine art, and quality ingredients also make it a great dining experience or stop-off for a late-night snack. **239 West 4th St., 646/449-9336, $$$**

■ **FOOD GALLERY 32**
Near the Empire State Building, this Korean food court houses independent stalls selling tasty noodles, rice dishes, soups, and stews. **11 West 32nd St., $**

WHIRLWIND TOURS

New York in a Weekend with Kids

Downtown

Visit the most imaginative museums and a bookstore where characters come alive.

3 The Lower East Side Tenement Museum (see pp. 30–31) Beginning in 1863, the modest apartment building at 97 Orchard Street was home to nearly 7,000 immigrants. Take a tour that recreates the life of a 14-year-old resident. Walk west along Delancey Street, then right on the Bowery, left on Spring Street, and right on Broadway.

4 The Scholastic Store (see p. 31) One of SoHo's best family destinations does more than sell books and toys. There are also interactive kiosks, crafts, games, and other activities guaranteed to please kids of all interests. Cross over to Spring Street and follow it west.

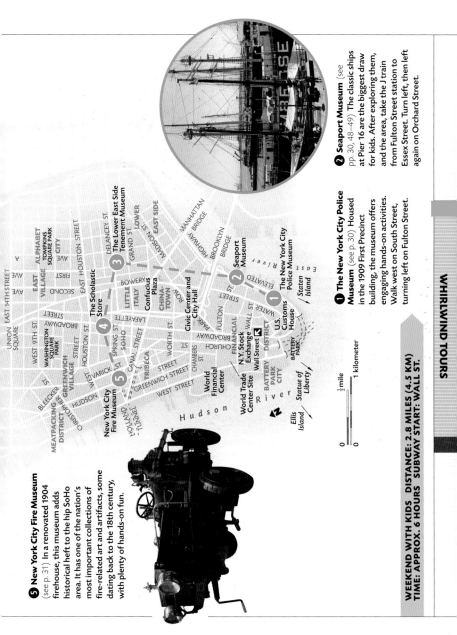

5 New York City Fire Museum

(see p. 31) In a renovated 1904 firehouse, this museum adds historical heft to the hip SoHo area. It has one of the nation's most important collections of fire-related art and artifacts, some dating back to the 18th century, with plenty of hands-on fun.

2 Seaport Museum (see

pp. 30, 48–49) The classic ships at Pier 16 are the biggest draw for kids. After exploring them, and the area, take the J train from Fulton Street station to Essex Street. Turn left, then left again on Orchard Street.

1 The New York City Police

Museum (see p. 30) Housed in the 1909 First Precinct building, the museum offers engaging hands-on activities. Walk west on South Street, turning left on Fulton Street.

Map labels

EAST 14TH STREET
UNION SQUARE
WEST 9TH STREET
EAST VILLAGE
ALPHABET CITY
TOMPKINS SQUARE PARK
AVE A
AVE B
FIRST AVE
SECOND AVE
WASHINGTON SQUARE PARK
GREENWICH VILLAGE
BROADWAY
EAST HOUSTON STREET
HOUSTON STREET
BLEECKER ST
CHRISTOPHER ST
MEATPACKING DISTRICT
HUDSON ST
WEST VARICK STREET
4 The Scholastic Store
LAFAYETTE ST
SPRING ST
SOHO
LITTLE ITALY
BOWERY
Confucius Plaza
CHINATOWN
DELANCEY ST
GRAND ST
3 The Lower East Side Tenement Museum
LOWER EAST SIDE
MADISON ST
MANHATTAN BRIDGE
CANAL STREET
5 New York City Fire Museum
TRIBECA
GREENWICH STREET
CHAMBERS ST
WORTH ST
WEST STREET
WORLD Financial Center
World Trade Center Site
BATTERY PARK CITY
Civic Center and City Hall
CHURCH ST
BROADWAY
WATER ST
FINANCIAL DISTRICT
N.Y. Stock Exchange
Wall Street
WALL ST
FULTON ST
SOUTH STREET
ELEVATED HIGHWAY
2 Seaport Museum
1 The New York City Police Museum
U.S. Customs House
BATTERY PARK
East River
BROOKLYN BRIDGE
Staten Island
HOLLAND TUNNEL
Hudson River
Ellis Island
Statue of Liberty
N

0   ½ mile
0   1 kilometer

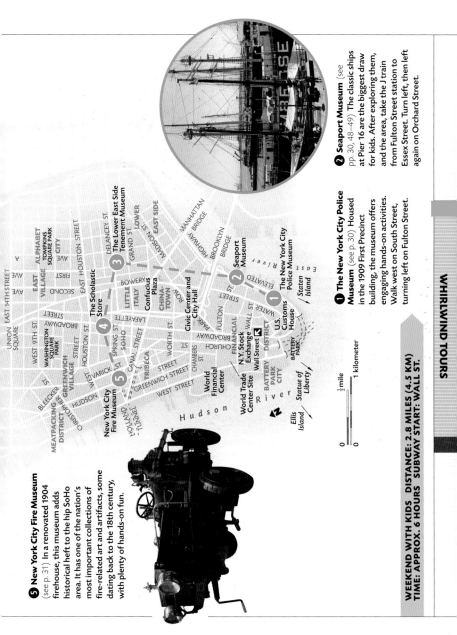

WHIRLWIND TOURS

WEEKEND WITH KIDS DISTANCE: 2.8 MILES (4.5 KM)
TIME: APPROX. 6 HOURS SUBWAY START: WALL ST.

The New York City Police Museum

1 At the tip of Manhattan, kids can discover the stories and traditions of the largest police force in the United States. In the **Junior Officers Discovery Zone,** they can climb into an Emergency Service Unit vehicle, learn radio calls, hop in a police car or give it a quick wash-down, dress up in uniform, examine their own fingerprints, and test their detective skills. They can even join in a lineup, have mug shots taken, and get a behind-bars experience in the jail on the second floor. Don't miss the collection of vintage weapons or the portraits of criminals from olden times.

100 Old Slip • www.nycpm.org • 212/480-3100 • $$ • Closed Jan. 1, Thanksgiving, Dec. 25, and some public holidays • Subway: 2 or 3 to Wall St.

GOOD **EATS**

■ **AMELIA'S DINER**
Refuel in SoHo with hot and cold sandwiches, mozzarella sticks, and chicken tenders. **110 Varick St., 212/925-5998, $**

■ **FAMOUS BEN'S PIZZA**
Another SoHo stop-off is especially famous for its wide variety of pizza toppings. **177 Spring St., 212 966 4494, $**

■ **JOE'S SHANGHAI**
Try this Chinatown restaurant for soup dumplings, sesame chicken, or Szechuan-style string beans. **9 Pell St., 212/233-8888, $**

■ **KATZ'S DELICATESSEN**
Drop by the ultimate Lower East Side deli for a sandwich, hot dog with fries, or knish. Portions are generous, so you could split one meal between two kids. **205 East Houston St., 212/254-2246, $**

Seaport Museum

2 If your kids love ships and history, head to the Seaport Museum, downtown on the East River. Indoors, landlubbers can pore over scale models of the *Titanic* and the Cunard Line's *Queen Mary,* and memorabilia from the days of luxury liners. Would-be seafarers should make for Pier 16, part of the museum where historic ships are moored. Climb aboard the 1908 *Ambrose* **lightship** or explore above and below deck on the four-masted barque *Peking* (1911), one of the largest —and last—merchant sailing vessels ever built.

12 Fulton St. • www.seany.org • 212/748-8786 • $$ for Ships Only tour • Closed Mon. • Subway: 2, 3, 4, 5, J, Z to Canal St.

The Lower East Side Tenement Museum

3 This museum is the real thing—a refurbished tenement building where many immigrant families lived. At the Visitor Center on 103 Orchard Street book the **Confino Family**

WHIRLWIND TOURS

Program tour. An actress plays 14-year-old Victoria Confino, a Greek Sephardic immigrant, who introduces visitors to her apartment. She arrived in 1916 to find the Lower East Side's dirty, crowded streets a sharp contrast with the lush farmland where she grew up. You can handle household objects and ask questions about her life.

103 Orchard St. • www.tenement.org • 212/431-0233 • $$$
• Closed Jan. 1, Thanksgiving and Dec. 25 • Subway: F, J, M, Z to Essex –Delancey Sts.

The Scholastic Store

Kids rule at this flagship store in SoHo. On the first floor, **interactive kiosks** engage older ones with the quest for The 39 Clues, brain-teasing I Spy, and always captivating LEGO. On board **The Magic School Bus** they can browse a superb selection of science books. Younger kids will feel at home among the toys and play items in **Clifford's Dog House,** or nestled under the big dinosaur with a book in hand. Special events are often held on weekends.

The Magic School Bus at The Scholastic Store invites kids to pore over colorful science books.

557 Broadway, between Prince and Spring Sts. • www.scholastic.com/sohostore • 212/343-6166 • Closed Thanksgiving and Dec. 25 • Subway: R, W to Prince St. or 6 to Spring St. or B, D, F, V to Broadway–Lafayette St.

New York City Fire Museum

In this revamped beaux arts firehouse in SoHo, kids can try on gear and see hand-pumped engines, four-wheel hose reels, a horse-drawn 1901 steam engine, and motorized vehicles of the 1920s. Historic tools on display include leather fire buckets, alarm boxes, and speaking trumpets. Actual firefighters are often present to instill fire safety tips and answer questions.

278 Spring St., between Varick and Hudson Sts.• www.nycfiremuseum.org
• 212/691-1303 • $$ • Closed Mon. and major holidays • Subway: C, E to Spring St. or 1 to Houston St.

DAY 2

New York in a Weekend with Kids

Uptown

The best views of the city set the scene for adventures in science and nature.

Jacqueline Kennedy Onassis Reservoir

CENTRAL PARK WEST

UPPER WEST SIDE

WEST 96TH ST.

AVE

BROADWAY

AVE

WEST 86TH STREET
Children's Museum of Manhattan

RIVERSIDE DRIVE

HENRY HUDSON PARKWAY

END

CENTRAL PARK WEST

American Museum of Natural History

New-York Historical Society

CENTRAL PARK

WEST 76TH ST.

MBUS

WEST 72ND ST.

Whitney Museum of American Art

EAST 72ND ST.

AVE

5 Children's Museum of Manhattan (see p. 35) Since 1973, this museum has offered fun and interactive exhibits focused on world cultures, healthy lifestyles, and the arts and sciences. After exploring, walk east to Central Park West, then south.

6 American Museum of Natural History (see pp. 35, 140–141) Founded in 1869, this museum continues to meet its lofty ambitions to serve as a guide to the universe, the natural world, and human culture. Travel to the depths of the ocean and into the infinity of space before dinner.

❶ Top of the Rock (see p. 34)

Zip up to the Observation Deck for exciting views of the city—point out the landmarks with your kids. Walk east along 50th Street, then north on Madison Avenue.

❷ Sony Wonder Technology Lab

(see p. 34) Create games, movie clips, and soundtracks, and discover how computer technology began—all for free. Walk up Madison Avenue and turn west along East 58th Street to Fifth Avenue.

❸ FAO Schwarz (see p. 35) One

of the world's most popular toy stores is also home to a scrumptious candy shop. Walk north on Fifth Avenue to Central Park South.

❹ Central Park Zoo (see pp. 35, 124)

Let your kids run off surplus energy in the park on the way to the zoo. Exit from Central Park West and take the 1 train from 66th St.–Lincoln Center to 86th Street. Walk south two blocks then turn left.

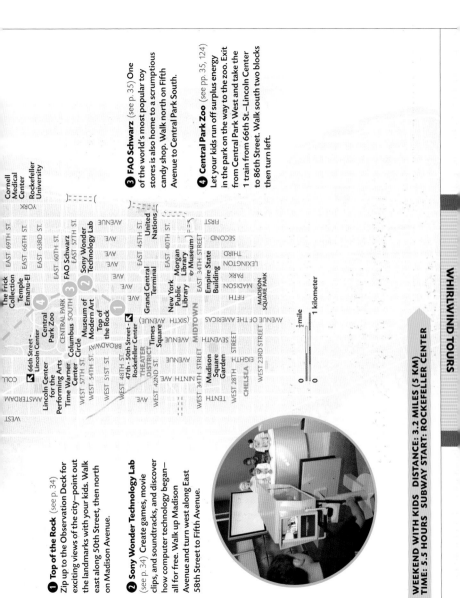

WEEKEND WITH KIDS   DISTANCE: 3.2 MILES (5 KM)
TIME: 5.5 HOURS   SUBWAY START: ROCKEFELLER CENTER

Top of the Rock

1 Towering above bustling Midtown, the Top of the Rock observation deck occupies floors 67, 69, and 70 of Rockefeller Center. An elevator whisks you up to the 360-degree views, which you can see from glass-covered terraces, or outside at the highest level, 850 feet (260 m) above ground. On a clear day, it's easy to spot the **Statue of Liberty.** Floor-to-ceiling windows make it easy even for little kids to see all around, and kids under six get in free.

30 Rockefeller Plaza • www.topoftherocknyc.com • 212/698-2000 • $$$$
• Subway: F, D, B, V to 47th-50th Sts.–Rockefeller Center

Sony Wonder Technology Lab

2 Begin on the fourth floor, at the **Login Kiosks.** Enter your favorite color and music, take your picture, and record your voice to create a unique digital profile to personalize exhibit experiences. At **Moviemaker,** choose clips and sound effects to make a movie trailer; the hilarious **Dance Motion Capture** exhibit shows animated characters performing your own dance movements. When you leave, you'll receive a certificate with all the stations you visited as a cool keepsake.

550 Madison Ave. at 56th St. • www.sonywondertech lab.com • 212/883-8100 • Closed Mon., Jan. 1, Thanksgiving, Dec. 25, and major holidays • Subway: 4, 5, 6, N, R to 59th St.–Lexington Ave., E, V, to Fifth Ave.–53rd St.

The Login Kiosks at Sony Wonder Technology Lab allow kids to personalize their visit.

FAO Schwarz

3 More than just the oldest toy store in the United States, FAO Schwarz is packed with games, gifts, and playthings from classic dolls to modern slot cars. It is also the home of the giant piano made famous in the Tom Hanks movie *Big*.

767 Fifth Ave. at 58th St. • www.fao.com • 212/644-9400
• Closed major holidays • Subway: N, Q, R to Fifth Ave.–59th St.

Central Park Zoo

4 Kids will love saying "Hi" to the animals that live in the Central Park Zoo, enormous polar bears and barking sea lions being favorites. Younger ones can get close to smaller animals at the **Tisch Children's Zoo,** a short walk from the main site, where they can pet goats, sheep, and pigs.

Fifth Ave. and 64th St.• www.centralparkzoo.com • 212/439-6500 • $$$ • Subway: N, R, W to 59th St.–Fifth Ave.

Children's Museum of Manhattan

5 The museum is organized according to kids' ages. Under-fives will enjoy educational fun with **Playworks** on the third floor. School-age kids should check out the first floor's changing exhibits and performances. The museum often features an exhibit with a lovable character, such as **Adventures with Dora and Diego.** Older kids will appreciate the fourth-floor displays, often on current themes in literature, such as mythology.

212 West 83rd St. between Broadway and Amsterdam Ave. • www.cmom.org • 212/721-1223 • $$ • Closed Jan. 1, Thanksgiving, and Dec. 25 • Subway: 1 to 79th or 86th Sts. or B, C to 81st St.

American Museum of Natural History

6 Don't miss the giant blue whale in the **Milstein Hall of Ocean Life,** life-size copies of a fossilized **prehistoric** *Barosaurus* mother and baby, and the **Rose Center for Earth and Space,** where the **Hayden Planetarium Space Show** delves into the origins of the universe. Advance ticketing is recommended and can be done online or on the phone.

Central Park West at 79th St. • www.amnh.org • 212/769-5200 • $$$ • Closed Thanksgiving, and Dec. 25 • Subway: B, C to 81st.–Museum of Natural History

GOOD **EATS**

■ **EJ'S LUNCHEONETTE**
This Upper West Side diner has delicious sweet-potato fries, grilled cheese, milk shakes, and more. Very kid-friendly, but you have to pay in cash. **447 Amsterdam Ave., 212/873-3444, $$**

■ **FIREHOUSE TAVERN**
Come here while on the Upper West Side for savory burgers, pizzas, fajitas, or burritos, and lots of decadent drinks and desserts. **522 Columbus Ave., 212/787-3473, $**

■ **ISABELLA'S**
After the American Museum of Natural History, try the kids' menu or a posh picnic-to-go at this spacious Mediterranean-style eatery. Reservations are recommended. **359 Columbus Ave., 212/724-2100, $$**

PART 2

New York's Neighborhoods

New York's Neighborhoods

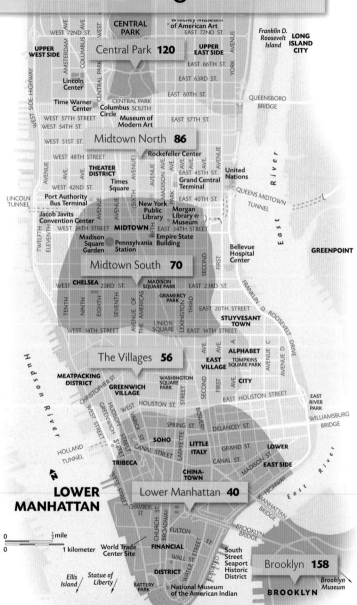

CENTRAL PARK

Whitney Museum of American Art

Franklin D. Roosevelt Island

LONG ISLAND CITY

WEST 72ND ST.

EAST 72ND ST.

UPPER WEST SIDE

Central Park **120**

UPPER EAST SIDE

EAST 66TH ST.

EAST 63RD ST.

Lincoln Center

EAST 60TH ST.

QUEENSBORO BRIDGE

Time Warner Center

Columbus Circle

CENTRAL PARK SOUTH

WEST 57TH STREET

WEST 54TH ST.

Museum of Modern Art

EAST 57TH ST.

WEST 51ST ST.

Midtown North **86**

WEST 48TH STREET

Rockefeller Center

THEATER DISTRICT

EAST 45TH ST.

United Nations

WEST 42ND ST.

Times Square

Grand Central Terminal

EAST 40TH ST.

QUEENS MIDTOWN TUNNEL

Port Authority Bus Terminal

New York Public Library

Morgan Library & Museum

LINCOLN TUNNEL

Jacob Javits Convention Center

WEST 34TH STREET

MIDTOWN

EAST 34TH STREET

Madison Square Garden

Pennsylvania Station

Empire State Building

Bellevue Hospital Center

GREENPOINT

Midtown South **70**

CHELSEA

23RD ST.

MADISON SQUARE PARK

EAST 23RD ST.

GRAMERCY PARK

EAST 20TH STREET

STUYVESANT TOWN

UNION SQUARE

WEST 14TH STREET

EAST 14TH STREET

The Villages **56**

ALPHABET

EAST VILLAGE

TOMPKINS SQUARE PARK

MEATPACKING DISTRICT

WASHINGTON SQUARE PARK

GREENWICH VILLAGE

CITY

WEST HOUSTON ST.

EAST HOUSTON STREET

EAST RIVER PARK

SPRING ST.

DELANCEY ST.

WILLIAMSBURG BRIDGE

SOHO

LITTLE ITALY

GRAND ST.

LOWER EAST SIDE

CANAL STREET

CANAL ST.

HOLLAND TUNNEL

TRIBECA

CHINA-TOWN

LOWER MANHATTAN

Lower Manhattan **40**

CHAMBERS ST.

FULTON

BROOKLYN BRIDGE

0 ⅓ mile

0 1 kilometer

World Trade Center Site

FINANCIAL

South Street Seaport Historic District

Brooklyn **158**

Ellis Island

Statue of Liberty

WALL ST.

DISTRICT

BATTERY PARK

National Museum of the American Indian

BROOKLYN

Brooklyn Museum

Hudson River

East River

Queens River

East River

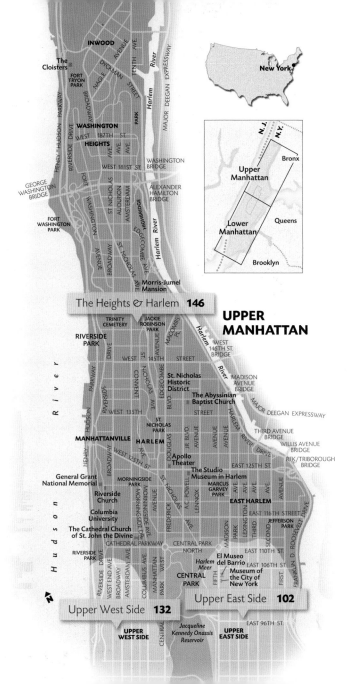

INWOOD

The Cloisters

FORT TRYON PARK

WASHINGTON HEIGHTS

WEST 187TH ST.

WEST 181ST ST.

WASHINGTON BRIDGE

GEORGE WASHINGTON BRIDGE

ALEXANDER HAMILTON BRIDGE

FORT WASHINGTON PARK

HENRY HUDSON PARKWAY

RIVERSIDE DRIVE

BROADWAY

DYCKMAN STREET

NAGLE AVE.

TENTH AVE.

AVENUE

Harlem River

MAJOR DEEGAN EXPRESSWAY

PARK

AUDUBON

AMSTERDAM

ST. NICHOLAS

HIGHBRIDGE

Harlem River

EDGECOMBE AVE.

ST. NICHOLAS AVE.

AVENUE

BROADWAY

Morris-Jumel Mansion

The Heights & Harlem 146

TRINITY CEMETERY

JACKIE ROBINSON PARK

MACOMBS PL.

WEST 145TH STREET

WEST 145TH BRIDGE

RIVERSIDE PARK

RIVERSIDE DRIVE

ST. NICHOLAS AVE.

CONVENT AVE.

EDGECOMBE BLVD.

St. Nicholas Historic District

The Abyssinian Baptist Church

MADISON AVENUE BRIDGE

WEST 135TH STREET

ST. NICHOLAS PARK

MANHATTANVILLE

HARLEM

WEST 125TH ST.

DOUGLAS JR BLVD.

AVENUE

AVENUE

AVENUE

Harlem River

Harlem River DRIVE

MAJOR DEEGAN EXPRESSWAY

THIRD AVENUE BRIDGE

WILLIS AVENUE BRIDGE

RFK/TRIBOROUGH BRIDGE

Apollo Theater

The Studio Museum in Harlem

EAST 125TH ST.

HENRY HUDSON PARKWAY

BROADWAY

MORNINGSIDE PARK

MORNINGSIDE AVE.

ST. NICHOLAS AVENUE

FREDERICK AVE.

AC POWELL BLVD.

LENNOX AVE.

MARCUS GARVEY PARK

EAST HARLEM

MADISON

PARK

LEXINGTON

THIRD

SECOND

AVENUE

FRANKLIN D. ROOSEVELT DRIVE

General Grant National Memorial

Riverside Church

Columbia University

The Cathedral Church of St. John the Divine

CATHEDRAL PARKWAY

CENTRAL PARK NORTH

EAST 116TH STREET

JEFFERSON PARK

EAST 110TH ST.

El Museo del Barrio

Harlem Meer

Museum of the City of New York

EAST 106TH ST.

RIVERSIDE PARK

RIVERSIDE DRIVE

WEST END AVE.

BROADWAY

AMSTERDAM AVE.

COLUMBUS AVE.

MANHATTAN AVE.

CENTRAL PARK WEST

CENTRAL PARK

FIFTH

MADISON

PARK

FIRST

Upper East Side 102

Upper West Side 132

N

UPPER WEST SIDE

CENTRAL

Jacqueline Kennedy Onassis Reservoir

UPPER EAST SIDE

EAST 96TH ST.

UPPER MANHATTAN

Hudson River

New York

N.J.

N.Y.

Bronx

Upper Manhattan

Queens

Lower Manhattan

Brooklyn

Lower Manhattan

Lower Manhattan technically constitutes everything below Houston Street and between the Hudson and East Rivers, but Tribeca and SoHo in the upper-west corner form artsy enclaves all their own. What really defines the area is the historic role it played in the founding of New York City and in turning it into a commercial power. At the tip of Manhattan, the Dutch purchased the island from the local Lenape people in 1626, and the city subsequently came under British control in 1664. Later, in 1785, New York became the first capital of the new nation following the Revolutionary War. The Statue of Liberty and Ellis Island in New York Harbor give some perspective on Manhattan as an island and offer a small reminder of New York's maritime history. But the most poignant effect Lower Manhattan has on the imagination may be as the site of the World Trade Center attacks of September 11, 2001. The rebuilding of the area is testament to the enduring spirit with which Lower Manhattan was settled centuries ago.

42 **Neighborhood Walk**

50 **In Depth: Statue of Liberty & Ellis Island**

52 **Distinctly New York: A City of Immigrants**

54 **Best Of: Downtown Shopping**

❹ **The Statue of Liberty arrived in New York Harbor in 1886, in 350 pieces. It was reassembled and dedicated in October of that year.**

Lower Manhattan

The packed neighborhoods of Lower Manhattan are diverse, merging immigrant culture with the bustle of Wall Street.

❺ Fraunces Tavern (see pp. 45–46)
The site of Washington's farewell address to the Continental Army in 1783 is a museum of pre-Revolutionary artifacts. Continue on Pearl Street and turn left onto Wall Street.

❹ National Museum of the American Indian (see pp. 44–45) Located in the grand rotunda of the 1907 Custom House, the museum presents Native American culture in rotating exhibitions. Turn right onto State Street, left onto Bridge Street, and cross to Pearl Street.

❸ Ellis Island (see p. 44) Visit the gateway to a new world for millions of immigrants. Return by ferry to Castle Clinton and cross the park to Bowling Green.

❷ Statue of Liberty National Monument (see p. 44) Take the ferry to Liberty Island, where France's gift is even more impressive up close— a museum in the statue's base tells the story. Continue by ferry to Ellis Island.

❶ Battery Park (see p. 44) Start at one of New York's oldest public spaces. Battery Park is the departure point for ferries to the Statue of Liberty and Ellis Island. Get tickets at Castle Clinton National Monument, the fort built for the War of 1812.

LOWER MANHATTAN   DISTANCE: 7 MILES (11 KM)
TIME: APPROX. 8 HOURS   SUBWAY START: BOWLING GREEN

LOWER MANHATTAN

Map labels:
TRIBECA
CANAL STREET
ROCKEFELLER PARK
Franklin Street
HUDSON
BROADW...
CHAMBERS STREET
Chambers Street
Chambers Street
BATTERY PARK CITY
VESEY
WEST STREET
WEST
World Trade Center
WORLD TRADE CENTER SITE
Cortlandt Street
Trinity Church
Rector Street
TRINITY PL
BATTERY PL
BATTERY PARK
To Ellis Island
To Statue of Liberty
Bowling Green
National Museum of the American Indian
Whitehall Street
South Ferry
To Governor's Island, Staten Island
City Hall
Park Place
Broadway
Nassau Street
Fulton Street
Fulton Street
Federal Hall National Memoria...
Wall St.
WALL ST.
Broad St.
Fraunces Tavern
WATER ST.
FINANCIAL DISTRICT
SOUTH

Map Labels

VARICK STREET
Spring Street
BROADWAY
SOHO
Canal Street
WEST BROADWAY
AVENUE OF THE AMERICAS
BROOME STREET
GRAND STREET
Canal Street
BROADWAY
Spring Street
LITTLE
KENMARE ST
SARA D. ROOSEVELT PARK
LAFAYETTE STREET
Canal Street
ITALY
Bowery
DELANCEY ST
Delancey Street
BROADWAY
Canal Street
Grand Street
Essex Street
CHINATOWN
BOWERY
CHRYSTIE
ALLEN STREET
LOWER EAST SIDE
WORTH STREET
COLUMBUS PARK
CANAL STREET
ESSEX STREET
SEWARD PARK
Chambers Street
FOLEY SQUARE
CHATHAM SQUARE
PIKE
EAST
EAST BROADWAY
CLINTON ST.
PARK ROW
Brooklyn Bridge-City Hall
ST. JAMES PLACE
MANHATTAN STREET
East Broadway
RUTGERS PARK
VIADUCT
SOUTH STREET
VIADUCT
BROOKLYN BRIDGE
MANHATTAN BRIDGE

East   River

10 South Street Seaport Historic District

0   600 meters
0   600 yards

– – – Ferry route

---

⑪ Chinatown (see p. 49) Peruse embroidered silk goods, exotic teas, and cheap watches; taste dumplings, noodles, and Peking duck to complete the day the Chinese way.

⑩ South Street Seaport Historic District (see pp. 48–49) Once America's center of commerce, the area still has tall ships in the harbor and offers plenty of great options for shopping, eating, and entertainment. Take the subway (J train) from Fulton Street to Canal Street at Centre Street.

⑨ World Trade Center Site (see pp. 48–49) Visit the site of the tragedy on September 11, 2001, and the memorial in the process of construction. Turn right on Broadway and left on Fulton Street.

⑧ Trinity Church (see pp. 47–48) With a museum, concerts, church services, and a graveyard, Trinity has been a place for contemplation for more than 300 years. Turn left up Trinity Place; Vesey Street is six blocks up on the left.

⑦ Federal Hall National Memorial (see pp. 47–48) Considered the birthplace of the U.S. government, this is where George Washington took the oath of office as the first president of a new nation. Walk along Wall Street to Broadway.

⑥ Wall Street (see p. 46) The center of the Financial District has a distinctly European feel with its crowded narrow streets—no surprise, since the Dutch settled the Wall Street area in the 1600s. Federal Hall is two blocks along on the right.

LOWER MANHATTAN

NEIGHBORHOOD WALK | **43**

Battery Park

① Dutch settlers landed here in 1623, erecting a battery of cannon to defend the pocket of land they called New Amsterdam. Today, gardens, sculptures, memorials, monuments, and recreation areas fill the 25 acres (10 ha) of downtown's largest public space. Enjoy waterfront views of the Statue of Liberty (see pp. 50–51), tugboats, barges, and sailboats. The park is also home to **Castle Clinton National Monument** (*www.nps.gov/cacl, 212/344-7220, closed Dec. 25*), a fort built to defend against a British invasion in 1812. It served as an immigration center before Ellis Island opened and now holds displays of historic Manhattan.

State St. and Battery Pl. • www.thebattery.org • 212/344-3491 • Subway: 5 to Bowling Green or 1 to South Ferry

SAVVY **TRAVELER**

A pedestrian paradise, the esplanade along the Hudson River runs the length of residential Battery Park City (Battery Park north to Stuyvesant High School). Transformed from urban scrub into a series of plazas, parks, and gardens, it has benches, picnic tables, and a path for strolling and jogging.

Statue of Liberty National Monument

② See pp. 50–51.

Liberty Island, New York Harbor • www.nps.gov/stli • 212/363-3200 • Closed Dec. 25 • Ferry from Castle Clinton National Monument in Battery Park • Ferry cost includes admission to the monument: $$$

Ellis Island

③ See pp. 50–51.

Ellis Island, New York Harbor • www.nps.gov/elis • 212/363-3200 • Closed Dec. 25 • Ferry from Castle Clinton National Monument in Battery Park • Ferry cost includes admission to the island and its sites: $$$

National Museum of the American Indian

④ Part of the Smithsonian Institution (an adjunct opened in Washington, D.C., in 2004), this branch resides in the George Gustav Heye Center, which occupies two floors of the 1907 beaux arts **Alexander Hamilton U.S. Custom House** at the

The National Museum of the American Indian has an archive of some 324,000 photographs.

foot of Broadway. Nearby Bowling Green is reputedly where the Dutch made a deal for Manhattan Island with the Native American inhabitants. Exhibits of literature, language, history, and the arts of American Indians are displayed in the splendid, elliptical **Grand Rotunda,** lit by a 140-ton (127 tonne) glass skylight.

1 Bowling Green • www.nmai.si.edu • 212/514-3700 • Closed Dec. 25
• Subway: 5 to Bowling Green

Fraunces Tavern

⑤ One of Manhattan's oldest buildings, this tavern was, by the 1760s, a popular meeting place for patriots, known as the Sons of Liberty. Here, in 1783, George Washington bade farewell to officers of the Continental Army. Today the site is a museum complex of four 19th-century buildings, plus the tavern, which was reconstructed in 1907. In addition to galleries of period paintings and re-creations of post-Revolutionary rooms that were once government offices, and more than 200 flags, the museum's highlights include a lock of George Washington's hair (reddish) and one of his false teeth—evidence that the ardent patriot, general, and first U.S. president was also a normal human being. The rustic Fraunces Tavern basement bar and restaurant, a branch of the Irish Porterhouse Brewing Company, is a good place for a pint and shepherd's pie for lunch. The huge selection of draught brews includes Oyster Stout (sweet and salty) made with fresh oysters simmered in the brew tank until they open up.

54 Pearl St., off Broad St. • www.frauncestavernmuseum.org • 212/425-1778 • $$
• Closed Sun., Jan. 1, and major public holidays • Subway: R, W to Whitehall St.

Wall Street

6 Pedestrianized since 9/11, Wall Street is home to the NASDAQ Stock Market and the New York Stock Exchange. Feel the pulse as office workers and stockbrokers buzz around, wheeling and dealing on their cell phones, even as they grab a quick lunch from food carts. The days of the wooden stockade built along this route by the governor Peter Stuyvesant to protect the new Dutch settlement, and for which the street is named, are long gone, but you can gain a more recent historical perspective at the **Museum of American Finance** (48 Wall St., www.moaf.org, 212/908-4110, $$, closed Sun., Mon., and major holidays). Here you can see a 60-pound (27 kg) gold bar from the Gold Rush, the ticker tape from the Great Crash, dated October 29, 1929, and the security features of paper money under ultraviolet light. An hour-long, reservation-only tour at the **Federal Reserve Bank of New York** (33 Liberty St., www.newyorkfed.org, 212/720-6130, closed weekends and bank holidays) includes a peek into the gold vault and entry to the bank's museum, where visitors can see money from all over the world.

Between Broadway and Water St. • Subway: 2, 3, 4, 5 to Wall St. or J, Z to Broad St.

LOWER MANHATTAN

Federal Hall National Memorial

7 Federal Hall is all about George Washington and "firsts." The bronze statue on the front steps marks the spot where Washington was inaugurated as president in 1789. This was the first capitol building of the new nation, where the first U.S. Congress met, and it was also the original City Hall of New York. The current building—an early example of Greek Revival architecture—was finished in 1842. Inside, visitors can see the Bible that Washington used for his oath of office, the railing against which he leaned, and the floor upon which he walked. Reproductions of colonial documents and currency are available in the gift shop. The broad steps outside offer a great view of the narrow historic streets of the nation's first capital city and of the frantic pace of business today.

26 Wall St. • www.nps.gov/feha • 212/825-6990 • Closed Sat., Sun., and major holidays • Subway: 2, 3, 4, 5 to Wall St. or J, Z to Broad St.

Trinity Church

8 This historic church was founded by Anglicans in 1697. Destroyed twice (by fire in 1776 and following heavy snow in 1839), the current church—built in the Gothic Revival style—dates from 1846. You enter through bronze doors sculpted with Biblical scenes similar to those on the Baptistry in Florence, Italy. Inside, the vaulted ceiling opens up the narrow space to a stained-glass wall above the altar. Prominent members of the congregation included Federalist Alexander Hamilton, who is buried in the churchyard. George Washington worshipped at nearby **St. Paul's Chapel** (*Broadway and Fulton St., www.trinitywallstreet.org/congregation/spc, 212/233-4164*), the only original colonial-era church in Manhattan. Thursday lunchtime concerts at Trinity by critically acclaimed

The soaring interior of Trinity Church displays many neo-Gothic elements: pointed arches, rib vaulting, and, above the altar, a brilliant stained-glass window.

GOOD **EATS**

■ CORTON
In Tribeca near Chinatown, exquisite French cuisine is served in an elegant dining room. **239 West Broadway, 212/219-2777, $$$$$**

■ JOE'S SHANGHAI
Soup dumplings and other Hong Kong-style delicacies make this spot a Chinatown legend. **9 Pell St. off the Bowery, 212/233-8888, $$**

■ MARC FORGIONE
Also in Tribeca, chef Marc "Forge" Forgione presents New American dishes in a former butter warehouse. **134 Reade St., 212/941-9401, $$$$$**

musicians provide an opportunity to rest and revive. Visitors may attend daily church services or take self-guided tours. But contrary to the 2004 movie *National Treasure*, you will find no elevator shaft to a secret room under the church.

Broadway at Wall St. • www.trinitywallstreet.org • 212/602-0800 • Subway: 2, 3, 4, 5 to Wall St. or J, Z to Broad St.

World Trade Center Site

9 Construction of the National September 11 Memorial & Museum is ongoing at the site of the World Trade Center tragedy. Plans include a **Freedom Tower** to honor those lost and two massive pools of water set within the footprints of the Twin Towers, with a park, five new skyscrapers, and a performing arts space in the surrounding complex. Get an overview of the project—expected to be completed in 2015—at the **Preview Site** (*20 Vesey St., www.911memorial.org, 212/267-2047*). At the **Tribute WTC Visitor Center** you can follow stories that unfolded that day and see the aftermath of the destruction.

Tribute WTC Visitor Center: 120 Liberty St. • www.tributewtc.org • 866/737-1184 • $$ • Subway: A, C, J, Z, 2, 3, 4, 5 to Fulton St. or E to World Trade Center or R to Cortlandt St.

South Street Seaport Historic District

10 Encompassing 11 square blocks around South and Fulton Streets, this district honors New York's maritime history. The **Seaport Museum** (*12 Fulton St., www.seany.org, 212/748-8600, $$$, closed Mon.*) tells the story of New York as a great world port. The collection includes scrimshaw, more than 1,000 ship models, and archives such as the last message from the captain of the *Lusitania* before it sank. The real draw is the collection of eight

The 1911 barque *Peking* (left) is one of the Seaport Museum's outdoor exhibits.

restored, historic ships at Piers 15 and 16 that include sail- and steam-powered vessels. You can even take harbor tours (*Thurs.–Sat., 212/748-8786, $$$$$*) aboard the tugboat *W. O. Decker.*

www.southstreetseaport.com • Subway: 2, 3, 4, 5, A, C, J, Z to Fulton St.

Chinatown

11 If you have time, explore Chinatown's heart—Mott and Pell Streets below Canal St. Visit the **Museum of Chinese in America** (*215 Centre St., www.mocanyc.org, 212/619-4785, $$, closed Tues. and Wed.*), where short films on Chinese Americans are shown. On Mott Street, visit **Ten Ren** (*No. 75*) to learn about tea and **Teariffic Café** (*No. 51*) for tastings. (See p. 23 for other dining options.)

www.chinatown-online.com • Subway: N, R, Q, J, Z to Canal St.

Statue of Liberty & Ellis Island

On a tiny island in New York Harbor many new arrivals became Americans, both in their hearts and by law.

A fresh wave of immigrants disembarks at Ellis Island circa 1915.

For the more than 12 million immigrants who crossed the Atlantic between 1892 and 1954, the first glimpse of their new home was a 165-foot (50 m) copper woman, green from oxidation and holding a torch of liberty. For many, the experience triggered abundant feelings of joy and hope. Their first steps on American soil took place just next door on Ellis Island, where they were checked and registered. Today, the descendants of these immigrants account for nearly half of the current population of the United States.

STATUE OF LIBERTY

Since 1886, this statue, with broken shackles at her feet and a tablet with the date of independence in her hand, has been an inspiration for Americans. A visit includes the **observation deck** and a **museum** in the pedestal. Here you learn the story of sculptor Frédéric-Auguste Bartholdi's creation, which was built with money donated by the French public and shipped across the Atlantic. Don't miss the famous lines from the poem by Emma Lazarus etched on the pedestal: "Give me your tired, your poor, / Your huddled masses yearning to breathe free."

Book months in advance for the highest possible access, to the **crown,** and take your ticket to the Information Booth before the security screening. Climbing the 354 spiraling steps is hard work, but if the exercise doesn't take your breath away, the views will.

ELLIS ISLAND

Greeted by stacks of luggage and photos, visitors to the **museum,** which is housed in the old immigration building of 1900, will immediately get a feel for what life was like for the new

arrivals. On January 1, 1892, 15-year-old Annie Moore from Ireland was the first immigrant to be inspected and have her details recorded. Millions followed from all over Europe, and exhibits outline the motives behind their journeys, from persecution and pogroms to lack of work. Artifacts, photographs, interactive exhibits, and oral histories convey the toll of travel and the difficult conditions that immigrants faced when they arrived.

At **The American Family Immigration History Center,** visitors can locate names of relatives at computer stations, or look up noted arrivals such as Albert Einstein. His details read: Landed April 2, 1921, Swiss ethnicity, resided in Berlin, left from Holland on *The Rotterdam*. A printout souvenir (suitable for framing) includes this kind of information and a photo of the ship.

Liberty Island and Ellis Island, New York Harbor • www.nps.gov/stli • www.nps.gov/elis • 212/363-3200 • Closed Dec. 25 • Ferry from Castle Clinton National Monument in Battery Park • Ferry cost includes admission to sites: $$$

A City of Immigrants

It would be impossible to imagine New York without its dynamic immigrant populations, visible, among other places, in the famous Lower Manhattan enclaves of Little Italy and Chinatown. Indeed, every group that has settled here, such as the Italian stonemasons and Eastern European tailors of the 19th century, has added to America's cultural heritage—while the city's diversity and the pace of immigration continue to increase.

LOWER MANHATTAN

Many immigrants lived in cramped Lower East Side tenements, one of which— 97 Orchard Street—is now a museum (above). Chinese New Year sees a dragon parade dance through Chinatown's main streets (right).

Cosmopolitan Origins

More than 36 percent of New York's population is foreign-born, and more than 800 different languages are spoken, making the city the most linguistically diverse in the world. The first arrivals in the Dutch-owned port town of New Amsterdam in the first half of the 17th century were Danish, English, Flemish, French, German, Irish, Italian, and Norwegian settlers. Many more followed, and by the early 19th century, New York was firmly established as the center of trade and opportunity in the New World. Political upheaval in Europe brought further influxes of immigrants. Between 1892 and 1954, more than 12 million arrivals passed through the Ellis Island immigrant inspection center (see pp. 50–51).

Melting Pot

The familiar "melting pot" term came from a 1908 play of the same name by the Anglo-Jewish activist and writer, Israel Zangwill. The term is somewhat misleading when considering New York, however.

The different ethnic groups that came to the city in the 19th and early 20th centuries did not meld, but clustered in neighborhoods that preserved their language, culture, food, and customs. Many lived in dangerously overcrowded tenements.

Harlem was a refuge for African Americans after the Civil War, while East Harlem, an Italian neighborhood until the 1950s, has since been transformed into a vibrant Latino enclave. There are hundreds more such pockets, some highly specific, where the wanderer can find food, conversation, literature, and people from every corner of the world. They include Little Senegal on 116th Street, where many people originate from French West Africa, and Little Odessa in Brighton Beach, a tiny fragment of Russia in Brooklyn.

ETHNIC **MUSEUMS**

Asia Society and Museum
A Rockefeller sculpture collection combines with film, dance, and concerts.
725 Park Ave. at 70th St., www.asiasociety.org, 212/288-6400, $$$

Italian American Museum
This converted bank in Little Italy also served as a center for new arrivals.
155 Mulberry St., www.italianamerican museum.org, 212/965-9000

The Lower East Side Tenement Museum
Take a guided tour (see pp. 30–31). **103 Orchard St., www.tenement.org, 212/982-8420, $$$$**

Downtown Shopping

Shopping in New York City is practically a contact sport, and nowhere is this more evident than in the boutiques and shopping throughways of downtown Manhattan. Stick to the main retail hubs below. Even if you're not buying, it's fun to see what trends are coming down the pipeline.

■ LOWER EAST SIDE

The Bowery marks the beginning of the Lower East Side, once home to a thriving Jewish community, today known for its nightlife and hip hotels. Boutiques around here trade in vintage cool. One such emporium is **Edith Machinist** (*104 Rivington St.*), with its artfully curated clothes and accessories. Also visit **Some Old Rubies** (*151 Ludlow St.*), a cozy little store selling customized vintage clothing. Appease kids (and yourself) with a trip to **Economy Candy** (*108 Rivington St.*) for throwbacks like Jujubes and Whatchamacallit bars. End the expedition with a cocktail at the **Hotel on Rivington**'s first-floor bar (*104 Rivington St.*).

■ SOHO

For both browsing and buying, SoHo is not to be missed. Peruse beautiful books at **Taschen** (*107 Greene St.*), custom-made Italian leather goods at **Il Bisonte** (*120 Greene St.*), colorful multicultural housewares at **Global Table** (*107 Sullivan St.*), and anime-inspired figurines at **Kidrobot** (*118 Prince St.*). Here, too, you'll find **John Varvatos** (*122 Spring St.*), award-winning designer of well-cut, unfussy menswear. On Broadway, shopping gems include **Pearl River Mart** (*No. 477*), an authentic Chinese department store that carries everything from traditional herbs to cheongsam dresses for toddlers.

■ NOLITA

Just east of Broadway lies Nolita (real-estate speak for "North of Little Italy"). Here, **Calypso Christiane Celle** (*407 Broome St.*) is a must for women. The store sells raw silk wrap dresses and handbags in buttery-soft leather. For outré fashion at similarly outré prices, visit **Opening**

Since 2002, Opening Ceremony has been selling quirky, upscale mens- and womenswear.

Ceremony (*35 Howard St.*), which brings together established and new designers, foreign labels, and vintage.

■ GREENWICH VILLAGE

Bleecker Street is ahead of the style curve with shops like **Intermix** (*No. 365*) for women's clothes and **Alexis Bittar** (*No. 353*) for jewelry. Since opening his boutique in 2001, Marc Jacobs has all but colonized the area—there's even a bookstore named **Book Marc** (*No. 400*). Prepare to be elbowed in the ribs by the perma-line of rabid shoppers at the tiny **Marc by Marc Jacobs Accessories** (*No. 385*).

■ MEATPACKING DISTRICT

Amid the warehouses, lofts, and nightclubs just south of Chelsea, you'll find high-end designer boutiques on and around 14th Street, adding yet more glamour to this once-gritty locale. They include **Stella McCartney** (*429 West 14th St.*) and the only free-standing **Alexander McQueen** store in New York (*417 West 14th St.*). The sartorial fun continues with the **Scoop** mini-empire (*861–875 Washington St.*) and insouciant French import, **Zadig & Voltaire** (*831 Washington St.*). Drop into the **Apple Store** (*401 West 14th St.*) for the latest must-have gadget.

The Villages

Famous for their colorful history, the East Village and Greenwich Village are linked but distinctive neighborhoods, bounded by 14th Street to the north and Houston Street to the south. The East Village, which stretches from Alphabet City in the east to Fourth Avenue and the Bowery in the west, was home to writers of the Beat Generation in the 1950s. With the rise of 1960s counterculture, hippies moved in where immigrants had once settled and created a new identity for this pocket of Lower Manhattan. Gentrification has brought in young professionals and families, but the East Village has kept its edginess and is still a great spot for an evening out. To the west, Greenwich Village combines a long tradition of bohemianism with some of the sharpest shopping and living spaces in its northwest corner, the Meatpacking District. At its heart, the area around Washington Square resounds with echoes of its literary past. Running from the Meatpacking District, the High Line—a park created from a former railroad—is a refreshing place to stroll and take in the views.

58 Neighborhood Walk
....
64 In Depth: Greenwich Village
....
66 Distinctly New York: City of Writers
....
68 Best Of: Jazz Clubs
....

❹ Street life in the East Village is relaxed and casual, in contrast to the elegance of uptown Manhattan.

The Villages

These neighborhoods reveal New York's literary and offbeat sides, with lots of places to relax and admire the scene—and the people.

THE VILLAGES

THE HIGH LINE

TENTH AVE

NINTH AVE

WEST

14th Street

8th Avenue

MEATPACKING DISTRICT

14TH

14th Street

6th Avenue

14th Street

EIGHTH AVENUE

ABINGDON SQUARE

GREENWICH VILLAGE

GREENWICH AVENUE

SOUTH

STREET

STREET

Hudson River

WEST STREET

GREENWICH STREET

STREET

CHRISTOPHER

Christopher St-Sheridan Sq.

SHERIDAN SQUARE

STREET

OF

VILLAGE SQUARE

WEST 8TH ST.

WASHINGTON SQ. N.

WEST 4TH ST

WASHINGTON SQUARE PARK

WASHINGTON SQ. S.

WASHINGTON SQ. W.

❻ The High Line (see p. 63) New York's only elevated park has some of the best views of the city, especially at sunset.

❺ Meatpacking District (see pp. 62–63) Trendy shops, clubs, and bars have transformed this area of former meat warehouses. Stop in at Chelsea Market, then make for the 14th Street entrance to the High Line.

HUDSON STREET

SEVENTH AVENUE

West 4th Street-Washington Sq.

WALKER PARK

WEST HOUSTON STREET

Houston Street

LA GUARDIA PLACE

WEST HOUSTON STREET

Broadway-Lafayette St.

0   600 meters
0   600 yards

**THE VILLAGES DISTANCE: APPROX. 5.5 MILES (9 KM)
TIME: APPROX. 7 HOURS SUBWAY START: ASTOR PLACE**

4 **Union Square Park** (see p. 62) New York's favorite farmers' market is held among statues of famous people in this park at the northeast corner of Greenwich Village. Head on toward the western end of West 14th Street.

3 **Greenwich Village** (see pp. 64–65) Ramble around this bohemian stronghold. From Washington Square, walk north on University Place.

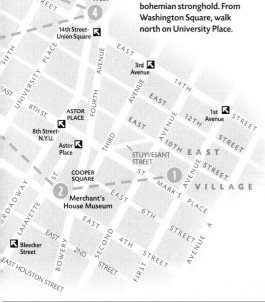

2 **Merchant's House Museum** (see p. 61) Lovingly curated rooms and furnishings offer a glimpse into 19th-century city life in this time capsule on the borders of the East Village and Greenwich Village. Continue west on West Fourth Street.

1 **East Village** (see pp. 60–61) Start by exploring the streets of this lively, artsy area. From St. Mark's Place, walk south on Second Avenue then west on East Fourth Street.

East Village

1 Once an immigrant neighborhood, the East Village acquired its distinctive feel in the 1960s as the haunt of artists, musicians, and hippies, and as the center of America's counterculture. Gentrification has erased some of the area's grittiness, but the neighborhood's artsy vibe is still evident in the graffiti-covered walls and independent stores. Street artist Jim Power has decorated almost all of the 80 lampposts with ceramics, mirrors, and glass: a new streetscape known as the **Mosaic Trail.**

At the heart of the village is **St. Mark's Place,** where vintage shops help keep the alternative spirit alive. One of the most famous, **Trash and Vaudeville** *(4 St. Mark's Pl.),* has been dressing rock stars and teenage rebels since 1975. St. Mark's Place ends at **Tompkins Square,** the scene of the first labor demonstration in 1874 and a performance space for Jimi Hendrix, The Grateful Dead, and other 1960s legends. Punk rock arrived in the 1970s, with bands

St. Mark's Bookshop, at 31 Third Avenue, has drawn East Village bibliophiles since 1977.

such as the Ramones and Blondie regularly playing at the (now defunct) CBGB nightclub on the Bowery, once the slummiest area of the city. The street's name derives from the *bouwerij* or farm belonging to the Dutch governor Peter Stuyvesant in the 17th century. He is buried at nearby **St. Mark's Church in-the-Bowery** (*131 East 10th St.),* one of New York's oldest churches. The East Village's Avenues A, B, C, and D—known as **Alphabet City**—have become a trendy enclave, with a nightlife that draws many uptowners. If you feel in need of refreshment in your wanderings, drop in at **Veniero's Pasticceria & Caffè** (*342 East 11th St.),* or **McSorley's Old Ale House** (*15 East 7th St.),* which dates to 1854.

Between East 14th and Houston Sts., and Broadway and Ave. D
• www.eastvillagevisitorcenter.com • 212/228-5335
• Subway: 6 to Astor Pl.

Merchant's House Museum

2 A wealthy merchant family, the Tredwells, owned this Federal-style row house, built in 1832—the city's only 19th-century home that retains its original interior and exterior. Displayed in eight rooms over three floors are the family's fixtures and furnishings, decorative arts, and personal possessions. Occasionally, one or two items from the Tredwell Dress Collection are on display. The museum is also reportedly Manhattan's most haunted house. Every October it presents Candlelight Ghost Tours; Gertrude Tredwell, the last owner, who died in 1933, is summoned from the great beyond.

29 East Fourth St., between the Bowery and Lafayette St. • www.merchants house.com • 212/777-1089 • $$ • Closed Tues., Wed., major holidays
• Subway: 6 to Astor Place

GOOD **EATS**

■ **CHELSEA MARKET**
This indoor market just north of Greenwich Village offers a huge range of gourmet food shopping, from delectable lobster to the perfect cup of coffee. **75 Ninth Ave., between West 15th and West 16th Sts., 212/243-6005**

■ **PRUNE**
Acclaimed chef Gabrielle Hamilton serves simple but sophisticated fare in this tiny, charming bistro. **54 East First St., between First and Second Aves., 212/677-6221, $$$$**

■ **UKRAINIAN EAST VILLAGE RESTAURANT**
Tap into the East Village's historic Ukrainian presence at this excellent folksy restaurant. **140 Second Ave., between East Ninth St. and St. Mark's Pl., 212/614-3283, $$**

Greenwich Village

3 See pp. 64–65.

Between Broadway and the Hudson River, and West 14th St. and Houston St.
• www.nycgv.com • Subway: A, B, C, D, E, F, V to West Fourth St.–Washington Square

Union Square Park

4 Marking Greenwich Village's northeastern tip, Union Square lies at the intersection—or union—of Broadway and Fourth Avenue. Its 6.5-acre (2.6 ha) park has a popular **farmers' market,** where you can sample local bread, cheese, wine, and crafts on Mondays, Wednesdays, Fridays, and Saturdays. During November and December, the **Union Square Holiday Market** takes center stage, with stalls selling everything from jewelry and candles to ornaments and Christmas décor. Among the famous sculptures dotting the park is a bronze equestrian statue of first U.S. President George Washington. Cast in 1814, it is the oldest sculpture in New York City's park collection. Be sure to look up at the surrounding buildings to spot the newest sculpted addition: the kinetic **Metronome** designed by artists Kristin Jones and Andrew Gizel. The piece features a digital clock and releases a continuous plume of steam.

14th St., at Broadway or Fourth Ave. • www.nycgovparks.org • Subway: 4, 5, 6, R, Q to 14th St.–Union Sq.

Meatpacking District

5 Once the home of the meat trade, this cluster of streets has transformed itself into Manhattan's trendiest quarter. Now it plays backdrop to some of the city's coolest restaurants, most exclusive clubs, and most expensive shopping. As you stroll the streets you'll see a few meatpacking houses surviving among the modern glass architecture, snapshots of the area's past. Along 14th Street you can window-shop at the high-end boutiques of Matthew Williamson, Jeffrey New York, and Yigal Azrouël. The tasty treats of **Chelsea Market** lie just to the north of the district. Its 28 upscale

Matthew Williamson's trendy clothes beguile shoppers at 415 West 14th Street.

food shops include Lucy's Whey for handcrafted American cheeses, and Eleni's for hand-painted cookies.

Between West 14th and Gansevoort Sts., and 10th Ave. and Hudson St.
• www.meatpacking-district.com • Subway: A, C, E, L to 14th St.–Eighth Ave.

The High Line

6 This unusual, slimline park, 30 feet (9 m) above the ground, was created along 1.45 miles (2.3 km) of disused freight track. Miniature landscapes, such as wildflower meadows and tree plantings, adorn the walking trail from Gansevoort Street to West 30th Street; en route you can pause on wooden loungers and viewing platforms, and peruse temporary art installations. With views of the Hudson River, the streets below, and surrounding neighborhoods, the High Line is a special place to watch the sun set over the city.

Access at Gansevoort and Washington Sts., and every 2–3 blocks running north
• www.thehighline.org • 212/500-6035 • Subway: A,C, E, L to 14th St.–Eighth Ave.

Greenwich Village

The neighborhood's radical, bohemian spirit has attracted some of the most creative minds in politics and the arts since the early 19th century.

Washington Square Arch commemorates the centennial of the first president's inauguration.

New York's regular street pattern breaks up around Washington Square, home of New York University since 1835 and hub of Greenwich Village. Known to locals as "the Village," the world-famous neighborhood originally really was a village. By the late 19th century, literary salons, art clubs, and cutting-edge theaters were flourishing; by the end of World War I, residents and visitors included avant-garde figures such as Marcel Duchamp. As you walk the streets, catch up with the Village's vibrant music and intellectual scene, past and present.

■ WASHINGTON SQUARE PARK

At the head of the 10-acre (4 ha) park stands the **Washington Square Arch,** completed in 1895. In 1917, members of the left-leaning Liberal Club, including artist Marcel Duchamp, scaled the 86-foot-tall (26 m) arch and proclaimed the "Independent Republic of Greenwich Village."

■ MUSIC & COMEDY

Since 1962, New York's oldest rock club, **The Bitter End** (*147 Bleecker St. at La Guardia Pl., 212/673-7030*) has been central to the area's music and comedy scenes. Bob Dylan, Stevie Wonder, and Woody Allen, among others, all performed here. **Café Wha?** (*115 Macdougal St., between Bleecker and West 3rd Sts., 212/254-3706*) also attracted major musical and comedy talents, including Jimi Hendrix, Bruce Springsteen, and Richard Pryor. Its house bands and guest musicians still pump out styles from jazz, soul, and R&B to modern and alternative. Don't forget to visit **Bleecker Bob's Records** (*118 West 3rd St., 212/475-9677*), the landmark record store with a selection of vinyl to suit all tastes. **The Stonewall Inn** (*53 Christopher St. at Seventh*

IN **THE KNOW**

The Village's Halloween Parade on October 31 attracts more than two million spectators every year, thanks to its 50,000 costumed revelers, variegated floats, giant puppets, and musical performances.

Ave., 212/488-2705) proclaims itself the birthplace of the gay liberation movement, after a police raid triggered the Stonewall riots of June 1969. Gay cabaret, karaoke, and comedy shows are all part of the lineup in the renovated bar.

■ WRITERS' VILLAGE

Close to Washington Square, charming **Patchin Place** was home to poet e. e. cummings, playwright Eugene O'Neill, and journalist John Reed. Drop in at cozy **Caffe Reggio** (*119 Macdougal St., 212/475-9557*) to sip a cappuccino where Jack Kerouac hung out. Theater lovers can sample New York's oldest Off-Broadway venue, **Cherry Lane Theatre** (*38 Commerce St., 212/989-2020*), where plays by F. Scott Fitzgerald, Tennessee Williams, and Samuel Beckett debuted. (See p. 23 for dining options.)

THE VILLAGES

Between Broadway and the Hudson River, and West 14th and Houston Sts. • www.nycgv.com
• Subway: A, B, C, D, E, F, V to West Fourth St.–Washington Square

City of Writers

From its early days, Greenwich Village has attracted some of the greatest names in American literature, including Mark Twain and Edgar Allan Poe. This phenomenon continued throughout the 20th century, while authors from around the world also swelled the throng. But ever since a native literature began to flourish on the continent, virtually every neighborhood in the city can claim to have housed a celebrated poet, novelist, playwright, or journalist.

Allen Ginsberg was snapped by his friend William Burroughs on their East Village apartment rooftop in 1953 (above). Before being colonized by writers, the White Horse Tavern (right) was a longshoremen's bar.

Beginnings

New York's literary roots can be traced to Washington Irving, considered the first American to make a living from writing. Famous for the short story "Rip Van Winkle," Irving was born and raised in post-colonial Manhattan. In 1807 Irving launched the satirical literary magazine *Salmagundi,* in which he coined the term "Gotham" as a pseudonym for New York.

Walt Whitman moved to Brooklyn with his family in 1824 and, by age 11, was working in the local newspaper business. After various travels outside of New York, he returned to Brooklyn and published his collection of free-flowing poems, *Leaves of Grass,* in 1855. His contemporary, Herman Melville, author of *Moby-Dick,* worked for many years as a New York City customs inspector.

Mark Twain was senior partner in the publishing company Charles L. Webster & Co., based in Union Square, until bad investments obliged him to file for bankruptcy. Having recouped his fortunes, he returned to New York in 1900.

Modern Greats

After World War I, wit and writer Dorothy Parker was the best-known member of the Algonquin Round Table, which met at the Algonquin Hotel (see p. 183). Her friend, Brooklyn-born humorist S. J. Perelman, was a regular contributor to *The New Yorker* magazine, founded in 1925. That year also saw the publication of *Manhattan Transfer,* John Dos Passos's novel inspired by New York life.

By the 1950s, New York was abuzz with literary talent, including poet Allen Ginsberg and novelists Jack Kerouac and Norman Mailer. Truman Capote published *Breakfast at Tiffany's* in 1958. James Baldwin published *Another Country,* set in Harlem and Greenwich Village, in 1962. In recent decades, figures such as the Bronx-born Don DeLillo and Brooklyn resident Paul Auster have dominated the city's literary scene.

LITERARY
WATERING HOLES

Kettle of Fish
Ginsberg, Kerouac, and friends spent many a happy night in this still popular neighborhood bar in Greenwich Village. **59 Christopher St., 212/414-2278**

Minetta Tavern
Opened in Greenwich Village in 1937, this now trendy restaurant once drew poet Ezra Pound and novelist Ernest Hemingway. **113 Macdougal St., 212/475-3850**

White Horse Tavern
In western Greenwich Village, the White Horse was a favorite with novelists Norman Mailer, James Baldwin, and Anaïs Nin. **567 Hudson St. at 11th St., 212/989-3956**

THE VILLAGES

Jazz Clubs

New York has been a magnet for jazz acts and aficionados since the early 20th century. From big bands in 1940s Harlem, to the bebop of the 1950s and 1960s, to innovators of avant-garde in the Village, the history of this lively music traverses the city from one end to the other.

■ GREENWICH VILLAGE & THE LOWER EAST SIDE

Arguably the most famous jazz club in the world, the **Blue Note** *(131 West Third St. between Sixth Ave. and Macdougal St., 212/475-8592) was* founded in 1981 and is the number-one choice for seeing big-name acts in an intimate setting. Just around the corner is **Village Vanguard** *(178 Seventh Ave. at Perry St., 212/255-4037)*, unmissable if only because it is where saxophonist John Coltrane made his famous 1961 live recordings. **Smalls** *(183 West 10th St. at West Fourth St., 212/252-5091)* promises an authentic club experience—a hole-in-the-wall basement space that presents up-and-coming talent. Over in the East Village, **The Stone** *(16 Ave. C at Second St., www.thestonenyc .com, closed Mon.)* is a not-for-profit space dedicated to avant-garde and experimental jazz.

■ MIDTOWN

One of the hottest Midtown clubs, **The Iridium** *(1650 Broadway at 51st St., 212/582-2121)* became famous for its weekly sessions with the late jazz guitarist Les Paul. You can still catch the Les Paul Trio on Monday nights, when world-class guitarists join them. Named for saxophonist Charlie "Bird" Parker, **Birdland** *(315 West 44th St., between Ninth and Eighth Aves., 212/581-3080)* carries on a 60-year tradition of bringing together big bands. For jazz with stunning scenery, head to **Dizzy's Club Coca-Cola** *(33 West 60th St. at Columbus Circle, 212/258-9800)* on the fifth floor of the Time Warner Center. It commands both a staggering view of Central Park and great jazz acts. Don't miss **Jazz Standard** *(116 East 27th St. between Lexington and Park Aves., 212/576-2232)*, where the Mingus Big Band plays most Monday nights.

THE VILLAGES

Guitarists Jeff Beck and Brian Setzer play at The Iridium as part of a tribute to Les Paul.

■ HARLEM

The historic heart of New York's jazz scene still boasts some of the city's best venues. Since opening in 1939, the **Lenox Lounge** *(288 Lenox Ave., between 124th and 125th Sts., 212/427-0253)* has hosted many greats, such as Billie Holiday, Miles Davis, and John Coltrane. An extensive renovation in 1999 has revived the glory of its early days. For a more intimate experience, try catching a jam session at **American Legion Post 398** *(248 West 132nd St., between Seventh and Eighth Aves., 212/283-9701)*. In a tiny basement of a brownstone, this friendly venue serves up excellent soul food, as well as accomplished jazz. (For more Harlem clubs, see p. 157.)

■ BROOKLYN

From Manhattan, a short hop on the F train to Park Slope in west Brooklyn takes you to French-owned **Barbès** *(376 Ninth St. at Sixth Ave., 347/422-0248)*, where hot world-beat jazz is often happening. Alternatively, amble over to the Fort Greene neighborhood, where **Frank's Cocktail Lounge** *(660 Fulton St., 718/625-9339)* is a Brooklyn institution, offering great live jazz on Thursday nights.

Midtown South

Midtown South runs between the two rivers and between 42nd and 14th Streets. During the boom years of the 19th century, this area was the city's commercial epicenter, and here the soaring Empire State Building and other art deco masterpieces rose into the air, forging both the modern skyscraper and the Manhattan skyline. There is much to delight the visitor at street level, too—the historic Gramercy Park neighborhood is great for a quiet stroll past stately brownstones and converted carriage houses. Fifth Avenue fashion emporiums rival the attractions of museums displaying rare artifacts. New York Public Library's marble lions protect a Gutenberg Bible and the real Winnie the Pooh; the Morgan Library & Museum houses the manuscript and art collection of 19th-century banker Pierpont Morgan; and the Rubin Museum of Art displays masterpieces from the Far East. For lunch, savor the city's finest spicy food in the Indian restaurants that line Curry Hill, the section of Lexington Avenue between 20th and 29th Streets.

72 Neighborhood Walk

80 In Depth: New York Public Library

82 Distinctly New York: A Passion for Fashion

84 Best Of: Bars & Cocktails

◀ **Madison Square Park provides one of Midtown South's peaceful places to slow down and admire the towering Empire State Building.**

Midtown South

New York's tallest skyscraper looms over this district of quiet parks, busy shops, and museums filled with priceless artifacts.

❶ Rubin Museum of Art (see p. 74) This museum of art from Himalayan countries houses a mask of the Hindu god Shiva in his fierce form. Make your way up Seventh Avenue, then west on West 23rd Street.

❷ Hotel Chelsea (see pp. 74–75) Writers and rock stars have called this bohemian hotel home. Head down West 23rd Street to Fifth Avenue.

❸ Flatiron Building (see pp. 75–76) The 285-foot-high (87 m) forerunner of the skyscraper tapers to less than 6 feet (2 m) wide at the front. Walk south on Broadway and turn right on East 20th Street.

0 — 600 meters
0 — 600 yards

**MIDTOWN SOUTH DISTANCE: 2.9 MILES (4.6 KM)
TIME: APPROX. 6.5 HOURS SUBWAY START: 18TH ST.–7TH AVE.**

MIDTOWN SOUTH

❽ New York Public Library (see pp. 80–81) The imposing marble building is home to one of the world's most extensive book collections.

GARMENT DISTRICT

HERALD SQUARE

Empire State Building

GREELEY SQUARE

MURRAY HILL

Morgan Library & Museum

MADISON SQUARE PARK

Gramercy Park

UNION SQUARE

STUYVESANT SQUARE

❼ Morgan Library & Museum (see pp. 78–79) Banker Pierpont Morgan's collection of cultural treasures includes rare manuscripts, books, prints, drawings, and paintings. Continue up Fifth Avenue to 42nd Street.

❻ Empire State Building (see p. 78) Manhattan's tallest building, this skyscraper affords sweeping views of the city. Farther up Fifth Avenue, turn right on East 36th Street.

❺ Madison Square Park (see p. 77) Spend some carefree time in this urban oasis of greenery. Follow Fifth Avenue north to East 34th Street.

❹ Gramercy Park (see pp. 76–77) This neighborhood features quaint town houses and architectural gems along tree-lined streets. From Park Avenue South, turn left on East 23rd Street.

MIDTOWN SOUTH

Rubin Museum of Art

1 The Western world's first and largest museum dedicated to Himalayan culture holds more than 2,000 items. They include pieces dating from the second to the 20th centuries from the mountainous regions between Afghanistan and Myanmar (Burma). A steel-and-marble spiral staircase winds up through the seven-story building to galleries that display Buddhist sculptures, vibrant Tibetan *thankas* (scroll paintings), ornate geometric paintings called mandalas, carved masks, and skillfully woven textiles. On the third floor, the exhibit "Masterworks: Jewels of the Collection" showcases outstanding works of art, such as a **14th-century Nepali Buddha;** a Tibetan bronze of a divine couple, **"Samvara in Union with Vajrayogini";** and photographic reproductions of the rarely seen **Lukhang Murals** in the temple of the Dalai Lamas in Lhasa, Tibet. At the **K2 Lounge** on Friday evenings, you can choose savory cuisine from a menu of Pan-Asian snacks while listening to music. Regular programs include film screenings and storytelling.

150 West 17th St., between Sixth and Seventh Aves. • www.rmanyc.org • 212/620-5000 • $$ • Closed Tues., Jan. 1, Thanksgiving, Dec. 25 • Subway: 1 to 18th St.–7th Ave.

Hotel Chelsea

2 During the 1950s and '60s, artists, musicians, and writers hung out at the Chelsea Hotel (popularly known as Hotel Chelsea) in what had become a bohemian commune. Originally built in 1883 as a private apartment cooperative, the 12-story, Victorian redbrick Gothic building with florid cast-iron balconies became a hotel in 1905. The famed venue has played host to such musical luminaries as Bob Dylan, Patti Smith, Jimi Hendrix, and Janis Joplin, as well as many writers—Arthur Miller and Gore Vidal among them. Songs, stories, and novels were written both in and about the hotel, including *2001: A Space Odyssey,* which Arthur C. Clarke penned while staying here. It was also here that years of heavy drinking caught up with the Welsh poet, Dylan

The Chelsea Hotel no longer accepts new long-term residents, limiting stays to just 24 days.

Thomas, who died after collapsing at the hotel following a visit to the White Horse Tavern in Greenwich Village. Perhaps the most infamous event was the murder of Nancy Spungen, possibly by her boyfriend—Sex Pistols bass player Sid Vicious. Rumors of ghosts, including Spungen's, have long swirled around the building; for a different kind of spirits, go to the **Chelsea Room** in the hotel's basement, where exposed brick and chandeliers set the scene.

222 West 23rd St., between Seventh and Eighth Aves. • www.hotelchelsea.com • 212/243-3700 • $$$ • Subway: 1, 2 to 23rd St.–7th Ave. or A, C, E to 23rd St.–8th Ave.

Flatiron Building

The triangular sliver of land formed by the intersection of Fifth Avenue, Broadway, and 23rd Street dictated the foundation for this oddly shaped structure, completed in 1902. Designed by Daniel H. Burnham & Co. (of Chicago World's Fair fame) and originally named the Fuller Building, this early skyscraper has a three-sided configuration that led to its current name—the Flatiron Building. A National Historic Landmark, it was one of the first structures constructed with a steel frame that formed a strong foundation for its exterior walls—an architectural principle employed in many later skyscrapers. Ornate geometric decorations are interspersed with terra-cotta faces that peer down at passersby. The Flatiron functions as an office building with stores on the ground floor, but the lobby has a photographic display illustrating its history.

175 Fifth Ave., between 22nd and 23rd Sts. • Subway: N, R to 23rd St.

Gramercy Park

4 This tree-lined neighborhood of architectural beauty was a swamp before it was laid out as one of New York's most attractive residential areas in 1822. The stretch of 19th Street between Irving Place and Third Avenue, with

its many mid-19th-century town houses, was dubbed the "Block Beautiful." It was once home to artists and writers including journalist Ida Tarbell. Elegant mansions grace the square: **The Players** club *(16 Gramercy Park)*—once residence of Shakespearean actor Edwin Booth (brother of Abraham Lincoln's assassin John Wilkes Booth)— was renovated by architect Stanford White. At 15 Gramercy Park, the **National Arts Club** is housed in a mansion once owned by New York governor Samuel Tilden. Prestigious club members have included writer Mark Twain, poet W.H. Auden, and sculptor Augustus Saint-Gaudens. The park that gives its name to the area remains closed to all but residents and Gramercy Park Hotel guests. Peek through the gates for a glimpse of its lush greenery. Saunter south one block for drinks at

Edwin Booth's popularity as the leading actor of his day survived his brother's notoriety, and he is honored in Gramercy Park.

Pete's Tavern (*129 East 18th St. at Irving Pl.*), one of New York's oldest bars, where writer O. Henry wrote his short story "The Gift of the Magi" in 1904. To the west is the **Theodore Roosevelt Birthplace**—a reconstruction of the house on this site where the U.S. president was born.

From 17th to 22nd Sts., between Park Ave. South and Third Ave. • Subway: 4, 6 to 23rd St. or 4, 6, N, R to 14th St.–Union Sq.

Madison Square Park

⑤ The vibrant, verdant ground that stretches from 23rd to 26th Streets between Madison and Fifth Avenues has been a dedicated public space since 1686. The six-acre (2.4 ha) park has a significant role in baseball's history; the city's first team, the New York Knickerbockers, formed here in 1845, before it opened as Madison Square Park two years later. Today, benches are set among shady trees, historic statuary, and year-round public art. **Bridget's Garden,** on the park's northern side, has a playground, while **Lilac Grove** brims with rare yellow primrose lilacs. If you're hungry, join the lines at **Shake Shack** (*Madison Square Park near Madison Ave. and East 23rd St, www.shakeshack.com, $*), on the southern end of the park, which serves burgers, a vegetarian Portobello creation, frozen custard, and of course, shakes, floats, and sundaes. In summertime, the **Oval Lawn Series** of concerts sends jazz, folk, and other music drifting through the air, all for free. There's also a free **Kids' Concert Series** on Tuesday and Thursday mornings in summer.

East 23rd to East 26th Sts., between Fifth and Madison Aves. • www.madisonsquarepark.org • 212/538-1884 • Subway: 6, B, D, F to 23rd St.

GOOD **EATS**

■ **BHATTI INDIAN GRILL**
Enjoy authentic North Indian cuisine, from spicy curries to savory kebabs, at this elegant upscale restaurant.
100 Lexington Ave. at 27th St., 212/683-4228, $$

■ **DHABA**
Savor Southern Indian food with dishes for vegetarians and meat-eaters alike.
108 Lexington Ave. between 27th and 28th Sts., 212/679-1284, $$

■ **PENELOPE CAFÉ**
A cozy café serving soups, salads, and sandwiches.
159 Lexington Ave. at 30th St., 212/481-3800, $

■ **PONGAL**
This small restaurant serves Indian cuisine at good prices.
110 Lexington Ave. at 26th St., 212/696-9458, $

Empire State Building

6 Until the Freedom Towers are completed in 2013, the instantly recognizable Empire State Building will remain New York's tallest tower, which it became once more following the 2001 terrorist attacks that destroyed the World Trade Center. Soaring 1,454 feet (443 m) into the New York City skyline, this art deco masterpiece, completed in 1931, reigned supreme for more than four decades as the world's tallest building. From scenes of King Kong scaling the structure to the poignant stories of *An Affair to Remember* and *Sleepless in Seattle*, it has provided a favorite backdrop for movie directors. Upon entering, stroll through the **ornate lobby,** where restored gold-leaf-on-canvas murals of the sun and planets grace the expansive ceiling. The walls feature painted panels of the Seven Wonders of the Ancient World. Amble over to the street level **Empire Room,** a large, upscale cocktail lounge. You can unwind here before taking the high-speed elevators to the **86th floor observatory,** or, for an extra fee, the **102nd floor observatory.** The last elevator leaves at 1:15 a.m., allowing for spectacular nighttime vistas of the millions of twinkling city lights.

350 Fifth Ave., between 33rd and 34th Sts. • www.esbnyc.com • 212/736-3100 • Observatory tickets: $$$$ • Subway: B, D, F, N,Q, R to 34th St.–Herald Square

Morgan Library & Museum

7 Financier Pierpont Morgan amassed an extraordinary collection of rare artwork, literature, and music memorabilia. Among its treasures are illuminated medieval and Renaissance manuscripts, a signed manuscript of a Mozart symphony, and the original copy of Milton's *Paradise Lost*. Such items are displayed on a rotating basis. Charles Dickens's manuscript of **A Christmas Carol** is always on view around Christmas, while permanent displays include **Ancient Egyptian tablets and seals** from 3000 B.C. onward. The fine art includes works on paper by Rembrandt and Peter Paul Rubens. In 1924, after the financier's death, his son J. P. Morgan, Jr., gave

The Morgan Library's rotunda has a marble floor and columns of Renaissance inspiration.

the library to the public. Housed in a 1906 Renaissance-style villa designed by Charles McKim, it has a **rotunda** with an ornately decorated ceiling and inlaid marble floor. The Morgan campus also includes a light-filled courtyard by noted Italian architect Renzo Piano that connects the library's three main buildings. Pause here to unwind, or attend a concert, lecture, or other live performance in the lower level **Gilder Lehrman Hall.** Casual dining awaits in the **Morgan Café,** or sit down to an elegant feast in the **Morgan Dining Room.**

225 Madison Ave. at 36th St. • www.themorgan.org • 212/685-0008 • $$$ • Closed Mon., Jan. 1, Thanksgiving, and Dec. 25 • Subway: 4, 5, 6 to 33rd St.

New York Public Library

8 See pp. 80–81.

Fifth Ave. at 42nd St. • www.nypl.org • 917/275-6975 • Closed all public holidays • Subway: 7 to Fifth Ave., 1, 2, 3 to 42nd St.–Broadway, or D, B, F, M to 42nd St.–Sixth Ave.

New York Public Library

See one of America's foremost libraries—with a Bible that changed the world and a bear who enriched countless children's childhoods.

The books lining the Rose Main Reading Room alone number more than 40,000 volumes.

A massive temple to all things literary, the Stephen A. Schwarzman Building—better known as the main branch of the New York Public Library—opened in 1911. As well as housing 8.7 million treasured artifacts and books, the library has one of the world's longest and most famous reading rooms, loved by writers such as Norman Mailer and Alfred Kazin. The beaux arts building, designed by architects Carrère and Hastings, was designated a National Historic Landmark in 1965.

THE LIBRARY LIONS

Standing guard at the library's entrance are Patience and Fortitude—marble lions designed by sculptor Edward Clark Potter and carved by a family of well-known marble cutters, the Piccirilli brothers. Mayor Fiorello LaGuardia gave the lions their names in the 1930s, after the qualities he felt New Yorkers needed during the Great Depression.

THE REAL WINNIE THE POOH

Although Christopher Robin named his cuddly toy Edward, it was as Winnie the Pooh that he became the world's most popular bear. The original stuffed animal, a first-birthday present from his father, A.A. Milne, resides in the **Children's Center,** with his friends Piglet, Eeyore, Tigger, and Kanga.

GUTENBERG BIBLE

Taking pride of place in the library's **Rare Book Division** is a Gutenberg Bible, printed around 1455. German publisher Johannes Gutenberg invented the printing press around 1440. Some 180 Gutenberg Bibles were originally produced, yet only 48 survive. The story goes that when this rare tome arrived from Europe, New York Customs House officials were required to remove their hats in honor of the holy book.

SAVVY **TRAVELER**

Don't miss the free, one-hour guided tours at 11 a.m. and 2 p.m., Monday through Saturday, and 2 p.m. on Sundays. Meet at the reception desk.

ROSE MAIN READING ROOM

Murals of pink-tinged clouds and sapphire blue skies embellish the ceilings of this 297-foot-long (90.5 m) room on the third floor, while daylight streams in through gracefully arched windows. At the room's entrance, the **McGraw Rotunda** has further murals depicting Gutenberg and other key figures in the history of books.

BRYANT PARK

Behind the building lies a verdant expanse used for the 1853 Crystal Palace Fair. The park provides multicolored blossoms, a twirling carousel, and numerous eateries. In summer enjoy a free concert, and in winter go ice skating or visit the holiday market (see p. 101).

MIDTOWN SOUTH

Fifth Ave. at 42nd St. • www.nypl.org • 917/275-6975 • Closed all public holidays • Subway: 7 to Fifth Ave., or 1, 2, 3 to 42nd St.–Broadway, or D, B, F, M to 42nd St.–Sixth Ave.

A Passion for Fashion

With many of the world's top designers making New York their home, the Big Apple offers fashion retail therapy like nowhere else. If you're passionate about what you wear, explore the haute-couture fashion houses along with numerous independent shops. You'll find famous names such as Calvin Klein, Vera Wang, and Marc Jacobs, while many of the smaller boutiques promise cutting-edge designs and new talent.

MIDTOWN SOUTH

Happy shoppers pause for a breath on legendary Madison Avenue (above). Louis Vuitton's opalescent store (opposite) adds a shimmer to a corner of Fifth Avenue.

Growing Fame

The Fashion (or Garment) District is a small neighborhood, running from 34th Street and Fifth Avenue to 42nd Street and Ninth Avenue. The area was originally known for manufacturing uniforms for sailors, farm workers, and Union soldiers during the Civil War. With industrialization and an improved economy came the demand for an industry to outfit American families.

By the early 20th century, factories here were making the majority of women's clothing in the United States. New York's first Fashion Week, which was held during World War II, drew attention to the new industry. Now the shows that make up Fashion Week are held twice a year, helping promote American designs to the world.

Stylish Education

The rise in the fashion economy led to the founding of the Fashion Institute of Technology (FIT) in 1944. Today, FIT is considered one of the world's top fashion schools, with alumni including Calvin

Klein, Ralph Rucci, and Reem Acra. The institute's museum displays garments from the 18th century to the present day *(Seventh Ave. at 27th St., www .fitnyc.edu, 212/217-4558, closed Sun. and Mon.).*

Fashion Shopping

Pay homage to Cartier, Gucci, Harry Winston, Louis Vuitton, Saks Fifth Avenue, Tiffany & Co., and many more iconic shops along **Fifth Avenue.** A trip downtown (see pp. 54–55) brings you to **SoHo,** where mainstream brands mix with stalls on Broadway selling handcrafted pieces. Along the **Bowery** in the East Village you'll find independent boutiques, such as Patricia Field *(302 Bowery, between East Houston and Bleecker Sts.),* owned by the *Sex and the City* stylist.

DESIGNER **STUDIOS**

Go straight to the source for skillfully crafted designer items.

Diane von Furstenberg
Call in at her one-stop shop for classic wrap dresses, shoes, and accessories. **874 Washington St. at 14th St., 646/486-4800**

Linhardt
Lisa Linhardt uses ethically sourced gems in her one-of-a-kind jewelry pieces. **156 First Ave. between Ninth and 10th Sts., 917/338-7822**

Michael Andrews Bespoke
Custom-designed menswear and a lavish bar provide good reasons to visit this cozy shop. **2 Great Jones Alley, off Great Jones St., 212/677-1755**

Bars & Cocktails

America's biggest city does socializing very well. Locals enjoy a brunch, power lunch, or post-work or pre-dinner cocktail, especially when it's artfully crafted. Whether you prefer a centuries-old tavern, a hidden underground den, or a rooftop lounge, there is always the perfect place to quench your thirst.

MIDTOWN SOUTH

■ CHIC & SLEEK

In Midtown South, Julie Reiner has created the menu at the art deco-esque **Flatiron Lounge** (*37 West 19th St., between Fifth and Sixth Aves., 212/ 727-7741*), where fresh juices and produce make the cocktails sing.

Upstairs at The Kimberly (*145 East 50th St., between Third and Lexington Aves., 212/702-1600*) is one of Midtown North's hidden gems. Relax in this rooftop lounge, presided over by mixologist Alex Ott, and enjoy a 360-degree vista of the city.

■ OLD SCHOOL

One of the city's oldest bars, Lower Manhattan's **Bridge Café** (*279 Water St. next to Brooklyn Bridge, 212/227-3344*) opened in 1794 in a former brothel and counted East River pirates among its patrons. Today, it's known for its Scotch selections and sumptuous soft-shell crabs.

■ INSPIRED SPEAKEASIES

Although forbidden cocktail dens are a distant memory of the Prohibition Era, speakeasy bars are not. Enter Greenwich Village's **Little Branch** (*22 Seventh Ave. South at St. Lukes Pl., 212/929-4360*), owned by mixologist Sasha Petraske, via an unmarked steel door. Downstairs, you'll find a dimly lit bar with knowledgeable tenders.

Once inside **Crif Dogs,** a hotdog shop in the East Village, you might think you've landed in the wrong place. Look a little closer though, and you'll notice a telephone booth leading to **P.D.T.,** which stands for "Please Don't Tell" (*113 St. Marks Pl., between First Ave. and Ave. A, 212/614-0386*). In this tiny underground bar, mixologist Jim Meehan has constructed an innovative menu featuring creative pairings such as bacon-infused whiskey with maple syrup and a twist of orange.

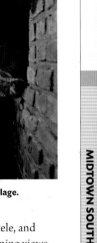

Cocktails are expertly mixed at the minuscule, subterranean P.D.T. in the East Village.

■ WINE & BEER

Long, banquet-style tasting tables set the tone in East Village's **Terroir Tribeca** (*24 Harrison St. at Greenwich St., 212/625-9463*). You'll receive your menu in a notebook filled with wine lists and amusing articles and political commentaries. Chef Marco Canora has fashioned a small-plates menu to complement the wines.

The cobblestone Meatpacking District gets a bit of whimsical fun at the **Biergarten** of **The Standard** hotel (*848 Washington St. at West 13th St., 212/645-4646*). Hotelier André Balazs combines ping-pong tables, sophisticated clientele, and plastic furniture with stunning views of the High Line—an elevated former railroad that has been transformed into a park (see p. 63).

Chef Daniel Boulud brings world-class wines to the Upper West Side at **Bar Boulud** (*1900 Broadway, between 63rd and 64th Sts., 212/595-0303*). You can sample from a carefully curated list of more than 50 wines, many from the Rhône Valley and Burgundy. Housemade charcuterie and Lyonnais-style dishes from chef Damian Sansonetti help the wines shine even more.

Midtown North

Midtown North touches both the Hudson and East Rivers, and is bounded by Central Park on the north and 42nd Street on the south. The sidewalks of this vibrant area bustle with office workers, shoppers cruising Fifth Avenue boutiques, and both locals and tourists flocking to Times Square's theaters and restaurants. Wall Street might carry New York's financial muscle, but the bulk of the city's corporate and cultural power is anchored in Midtown North, hub of publishing and broadcasting.

Much of what the nation reads and watches emanates from its steel-and-glass heights and neon-studded canyons. And worldwide, billions of people are affected by decisions made at the United Nations headquarters on the East River waterfront. The architecture demands your upward gaze at such world-renowned landmarks as the art deco Chrysler Building and Rockefeller Center. Representing the fine arts is the Museum of Modern Art, its recently expanded and renovated space a perfect showcase for its dazzling collection.

88 **Neighborhood Walk**

96 **In Depth: Museum of Modern Art**

98 **Distinctly New York: Art Deco**

100 **Best Of: Christmas**

◀ **The neo-Gothic twin spires of St. Patrick's Cathedral loom 330 feet (100.5 m) above Fifth Avenue, a captivating contrast to sleek skyscrapers.**

Midtown North

Walk from river to river to view magnificent skyscrapers, the city's glitzy theater district, and its unparalleled modern art collection.

MIDTOWN NORTH

❶ Intrepid Sea, Air & Space Museum (see p. 90) Veteran of three wars and the space race, the aircraft carrier *Intrepid* is the museum's centerpiece. Also on exhibit are a nuclear submarine and supersonic Concorde plane. Make your way five blocks east on 46th Street.

❷ Times Square (see pp. 90–91) Hub of New York's theater district, this major crossroads provides endless entertainment. From the south end of the square, walk east along 42nd Street.

❸ Madame Tussauds (see p. 92) Meet more than 200 lifelike figures of wax from the world of politics, sports, and the arts, including Lady Gaga. Backtrack through Times Square and go east on 49th Street.

**MIDTOWN NORTH DISTANCE: APPROX. 3 MILES (4.8 KM)
TIME: APPROX. 8 HOURS SUBWAY: 42ND ST.**

❹ Rockefeller Center
(see pp. 92–93) This city within a city includes the Top of the Rock observation deck, Radio City Music Hall, and, in winter, the celebrated ice rink in Rockefeller Plaza. Head north along Avenue of the Americas and then east along 53rd Street.

❺ Museum of Modern Art
(see pp. 96–97) The world's richest modern art trove, MoMA's collection spans Postimpressionism to cutting-edge digital expression. Walk half a block east along 53rd Street and then one block south on Fifth Avenue.

❻ St. Patrick's Cathedral
(see pp. 93–94) Manhattan's masterful Catholic cathedral provides a quiet respite from the Midtown mayhem. Continue south along Fifth Avenue and east along 42nd Street.

❼ Grand Central Terminal
(see p. 94) New York's temple of transportation bustles night and day with commuters and people who come to admire its vast expanses and beaux arts details. Continue east along 42nd Street.

❽ Chrysler Building (see p. 94)
Art deco meets the Age of the Automobile in the skyscraper with the silver spire, tallest building in the world until the Empire State Building was completed in 1931. Continue east along 42nd Street.

❾ United Nations Headquarters
(see p. 95) A monument to both modern architecture and aspirations to world harmony, the UN complex has been part of the East River skyline since 1952.

Intrepid Sea, Air & Space Museum

1 After serving in World War II, Korea, and Vietnam, the U.S.S. *Intrepid* (CVS-11) found a permanent home alongside Pier 86. Here it metamorphosed from a fighting machine into a wide-ranging museum devoted to mankind's achievements on the water, in the air, and even in outer space. Get up close and personal with nearly two dozen **military aircraft** on the carrier's flight deck and a supersonic **Concorde.** Test your aviation skills in an A-6 fighter-jet flight simulator, and relive the infamous day in 1944 when the carrier survived direct hits by two Japanese kamikaze planes. The space exhibits may seem out of place, but they are actually very relevant to the vessel's history: *Intrepid* served as the recovery ship on several Mercury and Gemini space missions. Visitors can tour the carrier on their own or join guided tours to see behind-the-scenes stops not accessible otherwise. Tied up beside the flattop (and also open to visitors) is the ***Growler,*** the world's oldest surviving nuclear missile submarine.

Pier 86, West 46th St. and 12th Ave. • www.intrepidmuseum.org • 877-957-SHIP (7447) or 212/245-0072 • $$ (includes admission to *Growler*), extra charges for simulator rides • Closed Mon. (Nov. to March), Thanksgiving, Dec. 25 • Subway: A, C, E to 42nd St.–Port Authority Bus Terminal

Times Square

2 Gazing up at the neon-lit billboards and theater marquees as a current of pedestrians and traffic swirls by, you have the overwhelming sense that Times Square really is the "Crossroads of the World." More than a million people gather each New Year's Eve to watch the Waterford crystal ball on the One Times Square skyscraper mark the start of a new year.

It's hard to imagine nowadays, but the square was once the outer edge of civilization, a collection of liveries and stables where many New Yorkers kept their horses and buggies. By the end of the 19th century, the first theaters had begun to appear, and by the early 20th century, this section of Broadway had been dubbed the Great White

Zoning ordinances require Times Square businesses to display illuminated signs.

Way (after its brilliant lighting). But over time patrons fled the area for other Manhattan temptations, and by the late 1960s, Times Square was the realm of dive bars, sex shops, and X-rated venues. In the 1990s a concerted effort by both public and private sectors revived the area.

Times Square glimmers once again as a place to shop, play, eat, or just watch the world walk by. Family-friendly attractions include the giant **Toys"R"Us** store *(1514 Broadway at 44th St.)* with its life-size animatronic *T-rex* and indoor Ferris wheel. Home to *Vogue, Vanity Fair,* and other fashion doyens, the new Condé Nast building *(4 Times Sq. between 42nd and 43rd Sts.)* adds a touch of class. **MTV**'s glass-fronted bastion *(1515 Broadway between 44th and 45th Sts.)* attracts hordes of eager teens. Tourists flock to the **TKTS discount ticket booth** in refurbished Duffy Square and elbow their way into local restaurants for quick pre-theater eats.

Intersection of Broadway and Seventh Ave. • www.timessquare.com • Subway: 1, 2, 3, N, Q, R to 42nd St.–Times Sq.

Madame Tussauds

3 This New York version of the venerable London waxworks does its best to keep pace with ever-changing pop culture. More than 200 wax creations are complemented by the "Scream" house of horrors with live actors (not for the squeamish), a Sports Zone with interactive games, and a "*Wizard of Oz* 4-D Experience" that includes a version of the classic movie packed with special effects.

234 West 42nd St., between Seventh and Eighth Aves. • www.nycwax.com
• 800/246-8872 • $$$$$ • Subway: 1, 2, 3, N, Q, R to 42nd St.–Times Sq.

Rockefeller Center

4 Oil fortune heir John D. Rockefeller, Jr., hatched the idea of a grand cultural, commercial, and entertainment complex on a large Midtown property he was leasing from Columbia University. The task of creating this "city within a city" was handed to Wallace K.

Harrison, whose team helped construct 19 buildings, ranging from immensely tall to surprisingly short, fronted by a plaza that would become a New York icon in its own right. The center's "front door" is on Fifth Avenue, the stubby Maison Française on the left and mirror-image British Empire edifice on the right. The flower-filled **Channel Gardens** in between provide a route into the heart of the center, culminating in **Rockefeller Plaza.**

Soaring straight up from the plaza, the 70-story **General Electric Building** reflects both the art deco vibe of the 1930s, when most of Rockefeller Center was built, and the boxy modernism of the postwar period. Affectionately called "30 Rock" by those who work within, the skyscraper was originally the home of the Radio Corporation of America (RCA), RKO Pictures, and NBC television. The lobby flaunts massive murals by Spanish artist José

Lee Lawrie's bronze art deco statue of Atlas is Rockefeller Center's largest sculpture, at 45 feet (13.7 m) tall.

Maria Sert, but the real attraction is the **Top of the Rock** observation deck *(www.topoftherocknyc.com, 212/698-2000, $$$$)* for its expansive views of Manhattan. **Radio City Music Hall** *(www.radiocity.com, 212/247-4777, stage door tours: $$$$)* is another part of Rockefeller Center worth visiting. With 6,200 seats, it ranks as the largest theater in the United States. The high-kicking Rockettes are among the acts that regularly perform here; behind-the-scenes "stage door" tours are a popular Radio City staple.

Avenue of the Americas between West 48th and 50th Sts.
• www.rockefellercenter.com • 212/332-6868 • Subway: B, D, F to 47th-50th Sts.–Rockefeller Center

Museum of Modern Art (MoMA)

5 See pp. 96–97.

11 West 53rd St. • www.moma.org • 212/708-9400
• $$$$ • Closed Tues., Thanksgiving, Dec. 25 • Subway: E, M to Fifth Ave.–53rd St. or B, D, F to 47th-50th Sts.–Rockefeller Center

St. Patrick's Cathedral

6 The seat of New York's Roman Catholic archdiocese and one of the nation's most renowned churches, St. Patrick's is a tribute to Irish Americans who played such an integral role in New York's history and to the can-do spirit of the 19th-century archbishop John Hughes. Ignoring criticism from wealthy patrons and poor parishioners alike, Hughes launched the project shortly before the Civil War on a patch of land that then lay well outside the city center. Architect James Renwick patterned the massive neo-Gothic structure after Germany's Cologne Cathedral. Although the church was consecrated in 1879, construction continued through the turn of the 20th century. Its twin spires were the tallest landmark along Fifth Avenue until the early 1930s, when

GOOD **EATS**

■ **THE OYSTER BAR**
Opened in 1913, this lavishly decorated train-station restaurant serves 24 types of oyster and numerous seafood entrées and platters.
Grand Central Terminal, 212/490-6650, $$$

■ **THE RINK BAR**
During the summer season, Rockefeller Center's ice rink morphs into an outdoor café-bar with cocktails, wine, and tasty finger foods.
30 Rockefeller Plaza, 212/332-7620, $$

■ **RUSSIAN TEA ROOM**
Founded by members of the exiled Russian Imperial Ballet in 1927, the Tea Room continues as a meeting (and eating) place for local writers, actors, and musicians from nearby Carnegie Hall.
150 West 57th St., 212/581-7100, $$

MIDTOWN NORTH

skyscrapers overtook the neighborhood. The 108-foot-high (34 m) nave can seat 2,500 people, and a number of its exceptionally rich stained-glass windows were made in Chartres, France.

Fifth Ave. between 50th and 51st Sts. • www.saintpatrickscathedral.org
• 212/753-2261 • Subway: E, M to Fifth Ave.–53rd St. or 6 to 51st St.

Grand Central Terminal

7 A masterpiece of beaux arts design, this steel, granite, and limestone building opened in 1913 as the city's state-of-the-art train depot. Outside, beneath the massive central window, a statue commemorates railroad tycoon Cornelius Vanderbilt. In the **Main Concourse,** the vaulted ceiling is decorated with the constellations of the zodiac, and as light streams through cast-iron windows and shadows move across the Tennessee marble floor, the space looks more like an ancient temple than a hub for transportation. The station's culinary offerings include five **gourmet restaurants** and a food court for casual, inexpensive dining.

87 East 42nd St. at Park Ave. • www.grandcentralterminal.com • 212/340-2583 or
212/532-4900 (train service info) • Subway: 4, 5, 6, 7 to 42nd St.–Grand Central

Chrysler Building

8 Art deco's fusion of the utilitarian with the artistic reaches its peak in the Chrysler Building. Automobile magnate Walter P. Chrysler funded the structure himself, working closely with architect William Van Alen. Although the 1,050-foot-high (320 m) building kept its "world's tallest" tag for only a year, its artistic merit has continued to soar. Many of Van Alen's architectural details were inspired by car motifs, including the stainless steel gargoyles, modeled after the radiator caps of a 1929 Chrysler. The building is best viewed from the observation deck of the Empire State Building, but visitors can also explore the art deco lobby, once a Chrysler showroom.

405 Lexington Ave. • Subway: 4, 5, 6, 7 to 42nd St.–Grand Central

MIDTOWN NORTH

The flags of United Nations countries fly in alphabetical order before the Secretariat Building.

United Nations Headquarters

9 A standout along this part of the East River, the building looks as modern today as it did upon its completion in 1952. American architect Wallace K. Harrison had overall design control of the project, but he consulted other maestros, including Brazil's Oscar Niemeyer and Le Corbusier from France, who devised the winning plan. The 39-story **Secretariat Building,** a masterpiece of post-modern skyscraper design, dominates the complex. Directly below is the futuristic **General Assembly** building, with its swayback roof and trademark dome. Guided tours start from the Public Lobby of the General Assembly building. Make time to browse the **gardens** with their river views, as well as diverse examples of modern art, including a 1950s Soviet sculpture, "Let Us Beat Swords into Plowshares," and a bronze monolith by Barbara Hepworth.

First Ave. at 46th St. • www.visit.un.org • Tours: Mon.–Fri. • 212/9963-8687 • $$$ • Closed all major holidays • Subway: 4, 5, 6, 7 to 42nd St.–Grand Central

Museum of Modern Art

MoMA, as it is affectionately known, houses one of the world's leading collections of art from the late 19th century to the present.

The sculpture garden, planted with beech and birch, acts as an outdoor room of the museum.

A few discerning women collectors, including Lillie P. Bliss and Abby Aldrich Rockefeller, founded MoMA in 1929. It became firmly established two years later with Bliss's important bequest of works from the Postimpressionist era, including a number by Paul Cézanne. Today, it holds more than 150,000 pieces of art as well as 22,000 film, video, and media works. The current building opened in 2004, its six floors nearly doubling the exhibition spaces, but the permanent collection still has to be shown in rotating displays.

THE POSTIMPRESSIONIST ERA

Highlights in the fifth-floor galleries include Vincent van Gogh's **"The Starry Night,"** painted while the artist was in a mental institution in St. Rémy, France, in 1889. Here, too, you will find Paul Cézanne's **"The Bather,"** also from the 1880s, and Pablo Picasso's 1907 portrait of five prostitutes, **"Les Demoiselles d'Avignon,"** which anticipated cubism.

SURREALISM & ABSTRACTION

Also on the fifth floor is surrealist Salvador Dalí's masterpiece, **"The Persistence of Memory."** Dalí drew inspiration from an overripe Camembert cheese to depict the melting watches in the painting. In **"Broadway Boogie Woogie,"** Dutch artist Piet Mondrian combined his trademark grid patterning with tiny squares and rectangles of color, suggesting the fast tempo of New York and his interest in jazz.

ABSTRACT EXPRESSIONISM & POP ART

The fourth floor displays the major figures of abstract expressionism. Jackson Pollock's classic "drip" painting,

SAVVY **TRAVELER**

Every floor at MoMA has a space for relaxation. In the central sculpture garden (once the site of founder Abby Aldrich's town house) enjoy a snack among works by Picasso, Auguste Rodin, and others. (See p. 22 for dining options.)

"One: Number 31, 1950," was created with the canvas laid out on the floor. Latvian-born Mark Rothko painted large, hypnotic canvases composed of rectangles of solid color, such as **"No. 3/No. 13"** (1949). Pop Art reflected the consumerism of the 1950s and '60s, using the imagery of the mass media, as in Andy Warhol's **"Campbell's Soup Cans"** (1962). Roy Lichtenstein's **"Drowning Girl"** (1963) has the melodrama of a comic strip frame, the speech bubble being part of the picture.

PHOTOGRAPHY

The third-floor collection covers the art form's entire history, including the work of Civil War photographer Matthew Brady. Dorothea Lange made poignant portraits of migrant workers during the 1930s, such as **"Migrant Mother, Nipomo, California."**

11 West 53rd St., between Fifth Ave. and Ave. of the Americas • www.moma.org • 212/708-9400 • $$$$; tickets include admission to same-day film screenings on the lower level • Closed Tues., Thanksgiving, Dec. 25 • Subway: E, M to Fifth Ave.–53rd St. or B, D, F to 47th-50th Sts.–Rockefeller Center

MIDTOWN NORTH

Art Deco

The robust lines and soaring spires of the Chrysler and Empire State Buildings were potent symbols of faith in the future, and they epitomize New York's love affair in the 1920s and '30s with the streamlined design of art deco. The style acquired official recognition at a 1925 exhibition in Paris: the "Exposition Internationale des Arts Décoratifs." The shorthand term "art deco" stuck, and the style influenced furniture, textile design, and the applied arts.

The marquetry elevator doors in the Chrysler Building's lobby (above), and its stainless steel stepped spire (right) display art deco style at its most magnificent.

Varied Inspiration

The style drew inspiration from many sources: the ancient civilizations of the Near East, pre-Columbian motifs from the Americas, modern European art movements such as cubism, and contemporary products of the 1920s.

Art deco was extremely versatile. Its sunbursts, chevrons, zigzags, trapezoids, and other geometric patterns could be applied to diners and jewelry, elevators and comic books, planes, trains, and automobiles. Most materials were well suited to its form—from newly invented aluminum and stainless steel to stone, wood, and terra-cotta. Not surprisingly, New York, the city of opportunity, fell for the new style and transformed itself into a science-fiction metropolis of silvery skyscrapers.

Neat Solution

Art deco also solved a problem introduced by the 1916 Zoning Resolution, which required that the niches, shelves, ledges, and rooftops on buildings be "stepped up" to the sky to allow a modicum of

MIDTOWN NORTH

sunlight to reach the streets below. Art deco gave these adjustments a decorative purpose, most brilliantly exemplified in the spire of the **Chrysler Building** (see p. 94).

Bold New Look

The **Barclay-Vesey Building** (*Avenue of the Americas between 41st and 42nd Sts.*), designed by Ralph Walker, was the first to represent the bold new look. Completed in 1927, the structure is crowned by a powerful, ornately decorated battlement, and it has ground floor bas-reliefs using the bell motif.

At the 1929 **Chanin Building** (*122 East 42nd St.*), artists Rene Paul Chambellan and Jacques Delamarre decorated the lobby and lower exteriors with bronze, glass, and terra-cotta. The Chrysler Building and **Empire State Building** (see p. 78) also share "high" art deco characteristics of lavishly decorated lobbies and entranceways. **Rockefeller Center** (see pp. 92–93) is another sublime example of the style, with decoration on lower levels, such as the ornate interior of Radio City Music Hall, while Lee Lawrie created superb deco sculptures and bas-reliefs for the public areas.

DECO **SHOPS**

Several notable Manhattan retail buildings exemplify art deco styling.

Bloomingdale's
59th St., between Lexington and Third Aves.
Opened: 1931

Hermès
691 Madison Ave. at East 62nd St.
Opened: 1929

Tiffany & Co.
727 Fifth Ave. at East 57th St.
Opened: 1940

MIDTOWN NORTH

Christmas

Beginning in late November, the holiday spirit in New York becomes contagious. From 34th Street north along Fifth, Madison, and Third Avenues and around Times Square, the air buzzes with excitement and the streets are laced with glowing lights and the aroma of roasted chestnuts.

■ HOLIDAY WINDOW DISPLAYS

In late November the giant department stores unveil their festive windows. Created by set designers and artists, these mini winterscapes and nostalgic interiors unfold before your eyes, along with whimsical holiday characters and remakes of Christmas movie scenes. The windows at **Macy's** in Midtown South (*151 West 34th St.*) and **Barneys** on the Upper East Side (*660 Madison Ave.*) are the most anticipated; **Lord & Taylor** (*424 Fifth Ave.*), **Saks Fifth Avenue** (*611 Fifth Ave.*), and **Bloomingdale's** (*1000 Third Ave. at 59th St.*) also join in the fun.

■ CHRISTMAS TREE LIGHTING CEREMONY

Every holiday season, a towering Norway spruce graces **Rockefeller Center** (see pp. 92–93). The tree, which averages about 80 feet (24 m) high, is dressed with more than 5 miles (8 km)

of lights and a Swarovski crystal star at the top. At the nationally broadcast lighting ceremony, usually held in late November, a lineup of singers and celebrities launches the festive season with carols and performances, as thousands fill the sidewalks to watch.

■ ICE SKATING

A special delight at this time of year is ice skating. Although many know about the ice rink at **Rockefeller Center** (see pp. 92–93), with its view of the holiday decorations and famous tree, there are other appealing options. Try Central Park's **Wollman Rink** (*59th St. and Sixth Ave., www.centralpark.com, 212/439-6900, $$$*), which offers skating lessons in addition to its magical winter wonderland views. At the park's northern end, you can also skate under the stars at **Lasker Rink** (*110th St. and Lennox Ave., 917/492-3857, www.central park.com, $$$*). Alternatively, head to

Christmas lights heighten the festive feel at Rockefeller Center's Ice Rink.

The Pond at Bryant Park *(West 42nd St. and Sixth Ave., 212/661-6640, http://thepondatbryantpark.com, skate rental: $$)* for a charming rink full of good cheer. Admission is free, and skating lessons are available. Complete your outing with a drink or meal at the Celsius restaurant that overlooks the Bryant Park rink.

■ HOLIDAY MARKETS
Pop-up shops and fairs become ubiquitous as shoppers start hunting for the perfect gifts. At **Bryant Park** *(www.bryantpark.org, 212/768-4242)*, you can sip hot chocolate and browse the numerous sparkling booths of the European-style market. The **Grand Central Holiday Fair** *(Grand Central Terminal, www.grandcentralterminal.com/go/mallevents.cfm)* offers everything from Italian ceramic tableware to handmade hats and scarves. Be sure to check out the light show in the main concourse. The **Holiday Market** at Union Square *(14th St. at Broadway)* pitches festive striped tents full of fun gifts, such as handmade jewelry and old-fashioned toys. The **Holiday Gift Shops** at St. Bartholomew's Church *(325 Park Ave. at 50th St.)* sell cold-weather accessories and handcrafted trinkets.

CARROLL AND
MILTON PETRIE
EUROPEAN
SCULPTURE
COURT

Upper East Side

The Upper East Side, extending from 59th to 110th Streets between Central Park and the East River, has been the neighborhood of choice for the city's wealthy elite since the late 1880s, which accounts for the many town houses, mansions, and upscale shops along the placid blocks from Fifth to Lexington Avenues. From Third Avenue extending east, the scene changes to newer high-rise apartments, although older brownstones can be found on the side streets. Now gentrified, these blocks were once German and Hungarian immigrant neighborhoods, and many of the churches and purveyors here will remind visitors of this heritage. The mayor's official residence, the 18th-century Gracie Mansion, is in Carl Schurz Park along the East River, where a riverside promenade is a peaceful change-of-pace. One stretch of Fifth Avenue has so many museums it is known as Museum Mile. A visitor could spend a week in the Metropolitan Museum of Art alone, so for a day's walk pick the top museums and seek out the key exhibits in each.

104 **Neighborhood Walk**

112 **In Depth: Metropolitan Museum of Art**

116 **Distinctly New York: Gallery Hopping**

118 **Best Of: Upper East Side Shops**

❍ **Large works from the 17th to the early 20th centuries grace the European Sculpture Court at the Metropolitan Museum of Art.**

Upper East Side

*Early 1900s mansions, fashionable shops, galleries, and museums
populate the Upper East Side between Central Park and the East River.*

⑤ The Jewish Museum
(see p. 109) The former
mansion of financier
Felix Warburg houses the
world's largest collection
of Judaica, with many
imaginative changing
exhibits. Walk up Fifth
Avenue to 103rd Street.

⑥ Museum of the City of New York
(see p. 110) Dedicated to New York
from its earliest days to the present, the
museum has an excellent photo archive
and period rooms, including John D.
Rockefeller's bedroom. Take the 4, 5, or
6 train from 103rd Street to 86th Street,
and walk to the end of the street.

**④ Solomon R.
Guggenheim Museum**
(see pp. 107–109) Frank
Lloyd Wright's building
contains a collection that
includes Postimpressionist
and abstract works.
Continue three blocks up

6 Museum of the
City of New York

5 The Jewish
Museum

6 96th
Street

K 103rd
Street

CENTRAL
PARK

EAST DRIVE

FIFTH

AVENUE

EAST 106TH STREET

EAST 104TH STREET

EAST 103rd Street

EAST 102ND STREET

EAST 99TH STREET

EAST 96TH STREET

AVENUE

AVENUE

AVENUE

CARNEGIE HILL

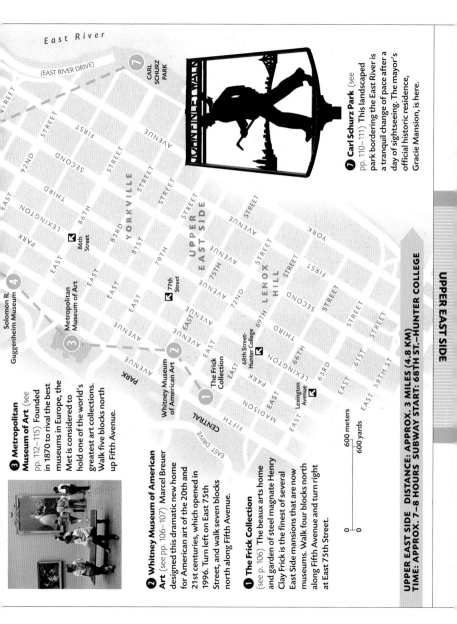

East River

(EAST RIVER DRIVE)

7 CARL SCHURZ PARK

92ND STREET

EAST 86th Street

YORKVILLE

UPPER EAST SIDE

4 Solomon R. Guggenheim Museum

3 Metropolitan Museum of Art

77th Street

Whitney Museum of American Art

2

LENOX HILL

1 The Frick Collection

68th Street-Hunter College

Lexington Avenue

CENTRAL PARK

EAST DRIVE

FIFTH AVENUE · MADISON AVENUE · PARK AVENUE · LEXINGTON AVENUE · THIRD AVENUE · SECOND AVENUE · FIRST AVENUE · YORK AVENUE

0   600 meters
0   600 yards

❸ Metropolitan Museum of Art (see pp. 112–115) Founded in 1870 to rival the best museums in Europe, the Met is considered to hold one of the world's greatest art collections. Walk five blocks north up Fifth Avenue.

❷ Whitney Museum of American Art (see pp. 106–107) Marcel Breuer designed this dramatic new home for American art of the 20th and 21st centuries, which opened in 1996. Turn left on East 75th Street, and walk seven blocks north along Fifth Avenue.

❶ The Frick Collection (see p. 106) The beaux arts home and garden of steel magnate Henry Clay Frick is the finest of several East Side mansions that are now museums. Walk four blocks north along Fifth Avenue and turn right at East 75th Street.

❼ Carl Schurz Park (see pp. 110–111) This landscaped park bordering the East River is a tranquil change of pace after a day of sightseeing. The mayor's official historic residence, Gracie Mansion, is here.

UPPER EAST SIDE

**UPPER EAST SIDE DISTANCE: APPROX. 3 MILES (4.8 KM)
TIME: APPROX. 7–8 HOURS SUBWAY START: 68TH ST.–HUNTER COLLEGE**

The Frick Collection

The mansion that steel magnate Henry Clay Frick (1849–1919) commissioned from the prestigious Carrère and Hastings architecture firm presents a rare opportunity to appreciate art in an intimate residential setting. Frick filled his home, completed in 1914, with 18th-century French furniture and porcelain, Oriental rugs, paintings, and sculpture, including an exceptional assortment of small bronzes. Holdings have been added, and since his death, the building has been enlarged, without losing its highly personal feeling. Paintings are not arranged by period, but rather much as they were when Frick lived here. Lovers of rococo art should seek out the Fragonard Room, where Jean-Honoré Fragonard's playful series "**The Progress of Love**" hangs. In the paneled Living Hall at the heart of the house, you will find masterpieces by Hans Holbein, Titian, and El Greco, while the sweeping West Gallery has a late **"Self Portrait"** by Rembrandt, Diego Velázquez's **"Philip IV of Spain,"** and Johannes Vermeer's **"Mistress and Maid."** Two other Vermeers hang in the South Hall—**"Girl Interrupted at Her Music" and "Officer and Laughing Girl"**—tracing Frick's interest in this enigmatic artist. The East Gallery mingles works by Francisco de Goya and Anthony van Dyck with Édouard Manet and Jean-Baptiste-Siméon Chardin. Finally, linger in the skylit **Garden Court,** an oasis of greenery.

1 East 70th St. at Fifth Ave. • www.frick.org • 212/288-0700 • $$$ • Closed Mon. and major holidays • Subway: 6 to 68th St. –Hunter College

A visitor contemplates Paolo Veronese's "Wisdom and Strength" at the Frick.

Whitney Museum of American Art

Sculptor Gertrude Vanderbilt Whitney (1875–1942) was an early patron and collector of works by contemporary American artists. When the Metropolitan Museum of

Art turned down her collection, she opened her own gallery in 1931 with some 600 works, including paintings by Thomas Hart Benton, George Bellows, Stuart Davis, Edward Hopper, Maurice Prendergast, and John Sloan. The museum continued to expand, and in 1966, it moved into its present modernist building designed by Bauhaus architect Marcel Breuer. In 1970, Edward Hopper's widow, Josephine, made a gift of more than 2,000 paintings, drawings, and prints by her late husband—the finest Hopper collection in the world. Today the Whitney holds 18,000 pieces by more than 2,700 American artists. Highlights include Edward Hopper's **"Early Sunday Morning,"** Jasper Johns's **"Three Flags,"** Alexander Calder's **"Circus,"** and Georgia O'Keeffe's **"Flower Abstraction."** The museum's Biennial exhibitions have surveyed recent and sometimes controversial developments in American art since Gertrude Whitney introduced them in 1932. Jasper Johns, Cy Twombly, and Cindy Sherman were among the artists to hold their first museum retrospectives here, and it was the city's first museum to present a video artist, with Nam June Paik's show in 1982.

945 Madison Ave. at 75th St. • whitney.org • 212/570-3600 • $$$
• Closed Mon.,Tues., Thanksgiving, and Dec. 25 • Subway: 6 to 77th St.

Metropolitan Museum of Art

3 See pp. 112–115.

1000 Fifth Avenue at 82nd St. • www.metmuseum.org • 212/535-7710 • $$$$
• Closed Mon. (except holidays), Jan. 1, Thanksgiving, Dec. 25• Subway: 4, 5, 6 to 86th St.

Solomon R. Guggenheim Museum

4 Without question, the Guggenheim's most famous exhibit is its own landmark building by the American architect Frank Lloyd Wright, as stunningly modernistic today as when it was completed in 1959. Wright's spiraling ramps show off art as few settings can. Exhibits have featured everything from master works to motorcycles. The permanent collection began with businessman and benefactor Solomon R. Guggenheim's own store of 600 "non-objective paintings" by abstract artists, such as Vassily Kandinsky and Rudolf Bauer. Forming part of this core collection are Kandinsky's **"Composition 8"** and Bauer's **"Invention (Composition 31)."** Guggenheim also sought out early pioneers of modern art with highly distinctive figurative styles. Examples include Amedeo Modigliani's **"Nude,"** Franz Marc's **"Yellow Cow,"** and Marc Chagall's **"Green Violinist."** A series of donations and purchases has since enriched the museum's holdings; the Justin K. Thannhauser bequest, for instance, added Impressionist and Postimpressionist masterpieces. Don't miss Paul Cézanne's **"Still Life: Flask, Glass, and Jug,"** Vincent van Gogh's **"Mountains at Saint-Rémy,"** and Pablo Picasso's **"Woman with Yellow Hair."** Other important acquisitions include works by Joan Miró and Paul Klee, and minimalist,

The Rotunda at the Guggenheim gives access to additional galleries in the adjoining Annex.

postminimalist, environmental, and conceptual work by contemporary artists such as Sol Lewitt, Donald Judd, and Bruce Nauman. The Thannhauser collection is on permanent view, while a donation by The Robert Mapplethorpe Foundation of 200 photographs usually appears as part of themed exhibits. Take the elevator to the top of the Rotunda and view the collections as you descend the gently sloping ramp.

1071 Fifth Ave. at 89th St. • www.guggenheim.org • 212/423-3500 • $$$ • Closed Thurs., Thanksgiving, and Dec. 25 • Subway: 4, 5, 6 to 86th St.

The Jewish Museum

5 This impressive museum, founded in 1904, chronicles the diversity of Jewish culture, both religious and secular. The French Gothic-style mansion of philanthropist Felix Warburg has housed the collections since 1947. It has been twice expanded and a sculpture court added to accommodate the vast holdings. These include some 26,000 objects that encompass paintings, sculpture, photography, archaeological artifacts, and ceremonial objects. A two-floor permanent exhibit, **"Culture and Continuity: The Jewish Journey,"** explores Jewish history through art, artifacts, video, photos, and TV excerpts, following the Jewish experience over 4,000 years, through harsh and tragic circumstances. Art here includes works by Elie Nadelman, Ben Shahn, Ross Bleckner, and Alfred Stieglitz. The museum also hosts temporary exhibits that have ranged from Paris salons to the Dead Sea Scrolls and celebrated Jewish luminaries in the arts.

1109 Fifth Ave. at 92nd St. • www.thejewishmuseum.org • 212/423-3200 • $$$ • $$$, free on Sat. • Closed Wed. • Subway: 4, 5, 6 to 86th or 96th St.

GOOD **EATS**

■ **CAFFE GRAZIE**
A charming setting, good Italian fare, and bargain lunch menu make this restaurant a top choice. **26 East 84th St., 212/717-4407, $$**

■ **CENTOLIRE**
Take your pick between Tuscan cooking in the restaurant upstairs and an informal café downstairs. **1167 Madison Ave., 212/734-7711, $$-$$$**

■ **DANIEL**
Daniel Boulud's very elegant home base is considered one of the city's finest restaurants. **60 East 65th St., 212/288-0033, $$$$**

■ **DAVID BURKE TOWNHOUSE**
The respected chef's flagship serves delicious American cuisine and prix fixe lunches. **133 East 61st St., 212/813-2121, $$**

UPPER EAST SIDE

Museum of the City of New York

6 The collections here got their start in 1923 as a small exhibit in Gracie Mansion (see opposite). This proved so popular that a Fifth Avenue site was found for a full-scale museum dedicated to New York's history and heritage. For a comprehensive understanding of New York, begin with **Timescapes,** a 22-minute multimedia experience, narrated by actor Stanley Tucci, that traces the city's growth from a settlement of a few hundred Europeans, Africans, and Native Americans to one of the world's great metropolises. Also on permanent view is a series of **New York Interiors** from the late 17th through early 20th centuries that gives a vivid picture of daily life, with furniture and decorative objects displayed in re-created room settings. The museum's enormous collections comprise some 15,000 paintings, prints, and maps, including the photography collections of Jacob Riis and Berenice Abbot, and more than 3,000 prints by the 19th-century printmaking firm of Currier and Ives. A menu of special exhibits completes the museum's attractions, which have benefited from a multimillion-dollar expansion adding three floors of gallery space.

SAVVY **TRAVELER**

The 92nd Street Y (*1395 Lexington Ave. at 92nd St., 212/415-5500*) **is one of the city's cultural hubs, home to a steady schedule of dance, music, poetry readings, and talks on politics and the arts.**

1220 Fifth Ave. at 103rd St. • www.mcny.org • 212/534-1672 • $$ • Closed Mon. (except holidays), Jan. 1, Thanksgiving, Dec. 25 • Subway: 6 to 103rd St. or 2,3 to Central Park North–110th St.

Carl Schurz Park

7 This hilly park spanning 14.9 acres (6 ha) overlooks the racing waters of the East River, at a section known as Hell Gate, where it meets the Harlem River and Long Island Sound. Stroll around the park to see the landscaping with ornamental stairs and lovely plantings, stretch your legs on the ten-block walkway along the river above East River Drive, or sit on a bench to contemplate the view. In 1798, Archibald Gracie (1755–1829), a Scottish-born

shipping magnate, bought property here for a country retreat, and he built his elegant mansion the following year. His parties were attended by such illustrious guests as President John Quincy Adams and future French king Louis-Philippe. In 1891, the city acquired the former Gracie estate, amalgamating it with the adjoining East River Park. The last of the country mansions that once lined Manhattan's East River shore, **Gracie Mansion** was the first home of the Museum of the City of New York and has served as the official residence of New York's mayors since 1942, when Fiorello La Guardia moved here. The park was named in 1910 for the German-born soldier, statesman, and journalist Carl Schurz (1829–1906), a move favored by the large German community then living in adjacent **Yorkville.**

East End Ave. at East 86th St. • www.nycgovparks.org/parks/carlschurz • Subway: 4, 5, 6 to 86th St. • Gracie Mansion: East End Ave. at East 88th St. • www.nyc.gov/gracie • Open for tours on Wed. only • $$ • 212/570-4751

Gracie Mansion, New York's oldest wooden building, is a model of early American style.

Metropolitan Museum of Art

The largest art collection in the U.S., the Met can be overwhelming so decide what to see before you go.

The Met has stood on its current site in Central Park since 1880.

At the Metropolitan Museum of Art, ancient Mesopotamia, 19th-century Paris, and 1960s New York are just yards and minutes away from each other. Founded in 1870 with the mission of collecting and exhibiting works that represent the "broadest spectrum of human achievement at the highest level of quality," the Met is one of the world's premier encyclopedic art museums. The sprawling galleries, spanning four city blocks, feature a collection drawn from six continents and covering eight millennia of world history.

■ Ancient Egypt

The first-floor Egyptian collection includes art and artifacts from the Old Kingdom to the era of Roman rule. Everyday objects appear alongside elaborate artwork made for the pharaohs and are a window into life along the Nile over thousands of years. Wood-carved models from **Meketre's Tomb,** circa 2000 B.C., function like miniature dioramas showing how this Theban official's estate operated and made him wealthy.

■ Greek & Roman Art

Beginning before the Geometric Period (900–700 B.C.) and ending in the Hellenistic (323–31 B.C.), this collection on the first floor comprises sculpture, glass, pottery, and wall painting. Among the stars is a beautifully painted **amphora** (two-handled jar) by the 6th-century B.C. Athenian potter and vase-painter Exekias. It shows four horses drawing a wedding chariot.

■ European Art

A meander around the first and second floors takes visitors from Renaissance Italy to Rembrandt's Amsterdam to van Gogh's adopted home in the south of France. Even in such distinguished company as this, there are standouts.

Pieter Brueghel the Elder's **"The Harvesters"** (1565), depicting wheatfields and peasants, is one of the first major paintings on a secular rather than religious theme. Diego Velázquez's **"Juan de Pareja"** is one of his few paintings of a non-royal subject.

■ Modern Art

The Lila Acheson Wallace Wing houses the Met's growing collection of modern art. Major works by modernist superstars include Pablo Picasso's **"Portrait of Gertrude Stein,"** Jackson Pollock's **"Autumn Rhythm,"** and Constantin Brancusi's **"Bird in Space."** Among the slightly lesser-known pieces are Romare Bearden's **"The Block"** (1971)—a collage of a tough New York neighborhood—and Marsden Hartley's **"Portrait of a German Officer"** (1914), created from metals, badges, and banners.

UPPER EAST SIDE

■ TEMPLE OF DENDUR

In The Sackler Wing, an intact temple, circa 15 B.C., from southern Egypt, is dedicated to the goddess Isis and two local deities. Wall carvings show the pharoah making offerings to the gods. The temple was built when Egypt was under Roman control, so the pharoah depicted is actually Caesar Augustus.

■ JOHN VANDERLYN PANORAMA

Painted panoramas became popular attractions in the United States in the 19th century. They were designed to surround the viewer, who had the feeling of standing in the location depicted. John Vanderlyn's circular painting of **Versailles,** in the American Wing on the first floor, transports visitors to a spot in the middle of the royal French gardens, surrounded by elaborate fountains, manicured hedgerows, and strutting monarchs.

■ GUBBIO STUDIOLO

Designed in circa 1476 for Federico da Montefeltro, duke of Urbino, the *studiolo* (little study) is a triumph in woodworking, on view in Gallery 501 on the first floor. The duke used

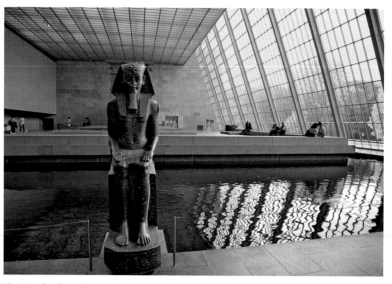

The Temple of Dendur once stood on the Nile, represented by a reflecting pool.

UPPER EAST SIDE

it as a personal haven in his palace at Gubbio, where he could study and think in peace. Using only wood inlay, the maker of this small room created a space lined with trompe l'oeil bookshelves and cabinets. He filled the shelves with the duke's favorite books, musical instruments, and scientific tools, also in wood inlay.

■ ROMAN CUBICULUM

The colorful *cubiculum* (Latin for bedroom) in Gallery 165 on the first floor comes from a place near Pompeii in Italy. Painted around 40–30 B.C., the **frescoes** show deities, altars with offerings to the gods, and objects such as trompe l'oeil glass vases. The eruption of Vesuvius in A.D. 79 buried the *cubiculum* in lava and ash, preserving the frescoes until they were excavated in the early 20th century.

■ ASTOR COURT

This indoor garden, installed in the second-floor Asian galleries, was built by a team of Chinese craftsmen in the early 1980s. They modeled it on a Ming Dynasty (1368–1644) scholar's garden. You enter through a moon gate (circular doorway) and continue

DON'T **MISS**

Millionaire Robert Lehman left a superb collection of works by Rembrandt, El Greco, and other great artists to the Met. See this often-missed area on the first floor in the Lehman Wing.

along a covered walkway. In one corner a small koi pond is surrounded by authentic Chinese *taihu* rocks— craggy, pockmarked limestone rocks that are prized elements of a scholar's garden. The Astor Court is always tranquil, a good place to pause during a day at the Met.

■ FRANK LLOYD WRIGHT ROOM

The American Period Rooms on the third floor include this living room by the 20th-century Chicago architect. Wright also designed and built the house it belonged to in a Minneapolis suburb around 1913. His signature features include low overhanging roofs and windows with geometric designs. The room was conceived in relation to the rural location of the house, and to evoke this original wooded setting, the museum installed the room so that it overlooks Central Park.

UPPER EAST SIDE

1000 Fifth Ave. at 82nd St. • www.metmuseum.org • 212/535-7710 • $$$$ • Closed Mon. (except holidays), Jan. 1, Thanksgiving, Dec. 25 • Subway: 4, 5, 6 to 86th St.

Gallery Hopping

New York's galleries are the most exciting in the United States. The city, which has long attracted many of the world's leading artists, is the focal point of the nation's art market as well as a major center of the international contemporary art world. Hundreds of New York galleries represent a huge range of artists, from established stars to the latest iconoclasts. The gallery scene is often a moveable feast, tending to follow the paths of artists.

UPPER EAST SIDE

Tom Otterness's "Mama Bear" (above) was shown by Marlborough Gallery at the 2011 Armory Show. In 2008 Chinese artist Ai Weiwei created "Illumination" (opposite) at the Mary Boone Gallery.

Around Midtown

After the Museum of Modern Art opened on West 53rd Street in 1929, the first cluster of important galleries appeared nearby on the upper floors of buildings around 57th Street. Early galleries, such as Peggy Guggenheim's Art of This Century, were the first to showcase the works of painters of the New York school, who included Jackson Pollock and Mark Rothko. Today's 57th Street still has prestigious contemporary galleries, such as **Marlborough** (*40 West 57th St.*), representing Fernando Botero and Red Grooms, and **The Pace Gallery** (*32 East 57th St.*), with Alexander Calder and Chuck Close.

Chelsea & the Lower East Side

In the 1990s, art dealers began to eye the lofty, low-rent spaces of Chelsea, running from West 18th to 27th Streets, between 10th and 11th Avenues. Until then, gas stations, garages, and warehouses were the area's main features. Now some 300 galleries line the streets or stack up in vertical "art malls"—buildings where the elevator opens to a different showroom on every floor. Chelsea is all about the avant-garde; its leading names include **Matthew Marks** *(522 West 22nd St.)*, **Sonnabend** *(536 West 22nd St.)*, **Mary Boone** *(541 West 24th St.)*, and **Gagosian** *(555 West 24th St.)*.

Another burgeoning area is the rapidly changing Lower East Side. In 2010, **Sperone Westwater** *(257 Bowery)* debuted in a modernist glass building with a room-size red elevator so eye-catching that people stop on the street to watch it ascend. The gallery represents artists such as Bruce Nauman, Tom Sachs, Susan Rothenberg, and William Wegman; its move here from Chelsea signaled the area's emergence as an art mecca.

THE **ARMORY SHOW**

The legendary 1913 Armory Show in New York City introduced European modern art that both shocked the public and influenced art making and collecting in the U.S. New York continues to attract important shows, including a modern version of the Armory Show each year in March.

Piers 92 and 94, 12th Ave. at 55th St., www.the armoryshow.com, 212/645-6440

Upper East Side Shops

The Upper East Side lures visitors with some of New York's most exciting shopping, from upscale designer boutiques to world-famous department stores, and books, accessories, gifts, and more in the many museum shops. Some of the price tags may be steep, but browsing is absolutely free.

■ DEPARTMENT STORES

Bloomingdale's *(1000 Third Ave. at 59th St.)* is rightfully famed as a trendsetter, its seven floors overflowing with the latest creations from famous label designers for men and women, as well as fine selections of cosmetics, housewares, gourmet foods, electronics, luggage, linens, and furniture. Two blocks away, ultra-chic, ultra-mod, ultra-expensive **Barneys** *(660 Madison Ave. at 61st St.)* prides itself on exclusive and avant-garde fashions and accessories. Its inimitable style also extends to home accessories and cosmetics.

SAVVY **TRAVELER**

The Italian menu at Fred's at **Barneys** *(212/833-2200, $$$)* is a favorite with sophisticated shoppers. At Bloomingdale's **Le Train Bleu** *(212/705-2100, $$)*, French dishes are served in the atmospheric setting of a Parisian train car.

■ MADISON AVENUE

The upscale blocks from 60th to 79th Streets on Madison Avenue are packed with shops featuring the world's top designers. A sampling of the long and distinguished list runs: **Calvin Klein** *(No. 654)*; **DKNY** *(No. 655)*; **Valentino** *(No. 747)*; **Giorgio Armani** *(No. 760)*; **Michael Kors** *(No. 790)*; **Emanuel Ungaro** *(No. 792)*; **Carolina Herrera** *(No. 802)*; **Moschino** *(No. 803)*; **Lanvin** *(No. 815)*; **Jil Sander** *(No. 818)*; **Dolce & Gabbana** *(No. 825)*; **Asprey** *(No. 853)*; **Yves St. Laurent** *(No. 855)*; and **Ralph Lauren,** with two fashion castles at *(No. 867)* and *(No. 888)*. Other luxury names include: **Bottega Veneta** *(No. 635)* for shoes and leather goods; **Christofle** *(No. 680)* for French crystal, china, and silver; **Frette** *(No. 799)* and **Pratesi** *(No. 829)* for fine linens; and

Glossy and replete with designer labels, Barneys began as a discount store in 1923.

Vera Wang (*No. 991*), if you see a bridal gown in your future. Jewelry shoppers with bulging bank accounts should investigate the block between 66th and 67th Streets for **Judith Ripka** (*No. 673*), **Fred Leighton** (*No. 773*), **David Webb** (*No. 789*), and **Breguet** (*No. 779*).

■ MUSEUM SHOPS

All the Upper East Side museums have shops with distinctive wares, but three are exceptional. Besides art posters and a huge array of books, the expansive shopping area at the **Metropolitan Museum of Art** (see pp. 112–115) has everything from jewelry and scarves to stationery and home décor, all in delightful taste. At **The Jewish Museum** (see p. 109) you can peruse quality china, candlesticks, frames, jewelry, and toys, many at reasonable prices. An adjunct **Design Shop** (*1 East 92nd St.*) sells jewelry and home accessories that are true works of art. For a display of books and appealing items with a New York theme (including a LEGO Rockefeller Center model), there's no better place than the shop at the **Museum of the City of New York** (see p. 110).

Central Park

Journalist Frederick Law Olmsted and architect Calvert Vaux designed the country's first landscaped park in 1858 to meet a need for urban greenery. In the 19th century, as ordinary New Yorkers searched for respite from the city, members of high society began pressing for a dedicated public space in which to socialize, and where the lower classes would benefit from fresh air. After a lengthy debate, an area of Manhattan unsuitable for commercial buildings was chosen as the site of the new park. Twenty thousand workers spent 20 years turning swamps into lakes, redesigning the rocky landscape, planting more than 270,000 trees and shrubs, and transforming the whole area into an idyllic pastoral oasis. Central Park (www.centralparknyc.org) stretches south to north from 59th Street to 110th Street and across from Fifth Avenue to Central Park West. The land on which it stands is estimated to be worth at least $528,783,552,000. Inside the park you can swim, ice skate, go boating, cycle, walk, or just enjoy the many lovely gardens.

122 **Neighborhood Walk**

128 **Distinctly New York: The City's the Star**

130 **Best Of: Outdoor Activities**

◗ Seen from above, the park's 843 acres (341 ha) form a vast verdant area—a stark contrast to the density of the skyscrapers that surround it.

Central Park

Among the attractions in the city's premier green space are gardens, lakes, a Gothic castle, and a memorial to former Beatle John Lennon.

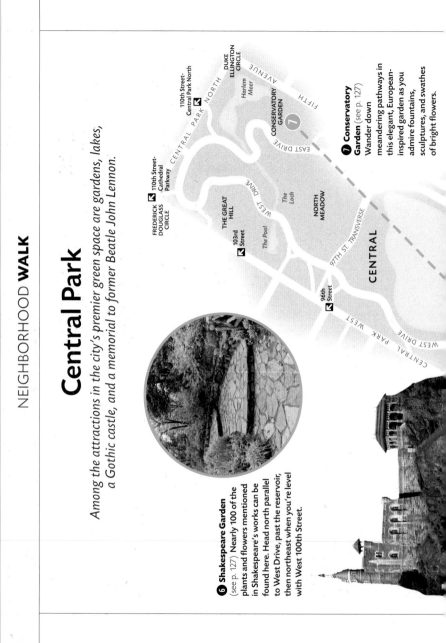

6 Shakespeare Garden
(see p. 127) Nearly 100 of the plants and flowers mentioned in Shakespeare's works can be found here. Head north parallel to West Drive, past the reservoir, then northeast when you're level with West 100th Street.

7 Conservatory Garden (see p. 127) Wander down meandering pathways in this elegant, European-inspired garden as you admire fountains, sculptures, and swathes of bright flowers.

FREDERICK DOUGLASS CIRCLE

110th Street-Cathedral Parkway

110th Street-Central Park North

CENTRAL PARK NORTH

DUKE ELLINGTON CIRCLE

Harlem Meer

CONSERVATORY GARDEN

FIFTH AVENUE

EAST DRIVE

THE GREAT HILL

103rd Street

WEST DRIVE

The Loch

The Pool

NORTH MEADOW

96th Street

97TH ST. TRANSVERSE

CENTRAL

CENTRAL PARK WEST

WEST DRIVE

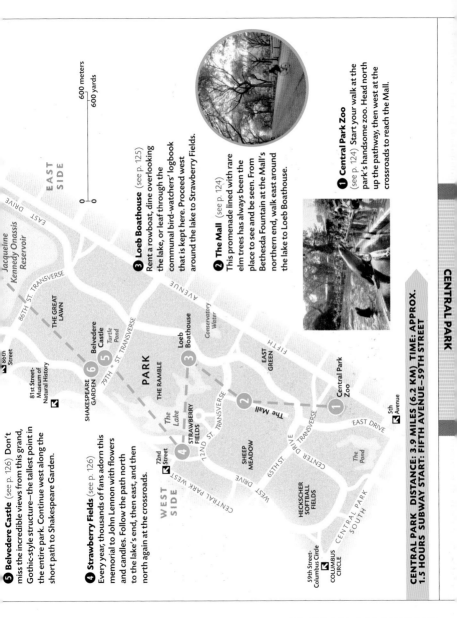

5 Belvedere Castle (see p. 126) Don't miss the incredible views from this grand, Gothic-style structure—the tallest point in the entire park. Continue west along the short path to Shakespeare Garden.

4 Strawberry Fields (see p. 126) Every year, thousands of fans adorn this memorial to John Lennon with flowers and candles. Follow the path north to the lake's end, then east, and then north again at the crossroads.

3 Loeb Boathouse (see p. 125) Rent a rowboat, dine overlooking the lake, or leaf through the communal bird-watchers' logbook that is kept here. Proceed west around the lake to Strawberry Fields.

2 The Mall (see p. 124) This promenade lined with rare elm trees has always been the place to see and be seen. From Bethesda Fountain at the Mall's northern end, walk east around the lake to Loeb Boathouse.

1 Central Park Zoo (see p. 124) Start your walk at the park's handsome zoo. Head north up the pathway, then west at the crossroads to reach the Mall.

CENTRAL PARK DISTANCE: 3.9 MILES (6.2 KM) TIME: APPROX. 1.5 HOURS SUBWAY START: FIFTH AVENUE–59TH STREET

Central Park Zoo

1 More than 150 species from around the world live in the Central Park Zoo, including red pandas, polar bears, and three rare snow leopards. The modern 5-acre (2 ha) facility was first established as a makeshift menagerie in 1860, expanded in the 1930s, and refurbished in 1984. Among its highlights are the octagonal sea lion pool in the central courtyard, where daily feedings take place, and the **Tisch Children's Zoo,** which opened in 1997, and where kids get the chance to pet and feed goats, alpacas, Vietnamese pot-bellied pigs, and more. Preservationists will delight at seeing the limestone friezes of birds, monkeys, and lions— vestiges of the 1930s-era zoo that was built to replace the menagerie. The **Delacorte Clock** will enchant all with its parade of brass animals circling to the tunes of nursery rhymes every half-hour.

Fifth Ave. and 64th St. • www.centralparkzoo.com • 212/439-6500 • $$$
• Subway: N, R, W to 59th St.–5th Ave.

The Mall

2 This long, tree-lined pedestrian walkway is the spot where New Yorkers used to come to stroll in their Sunday best, and it is still a great place for people-watching. It is flanked by benches and rows of giant American elms forming a leafy canopy, enticing many photographers into trying to capture the perfect Central Park shot. Not only visually stunning, the Mall's majestic trees also form one of the largest remaining collections of American elms in the country; the rest of the population has been nearly wiped out by Dutch elm disease. **Literary Walk,** at the southern end of the promenade, displays five bronze statues of famous writers, including William Shakespeare and Scottish poet Robert Burns; the other end of the walkway culminates at **Bethesda Terrace,** an ornately carved overlook with views of the lake and the wooded Ramble beyond.

Mid-park from 66th to 72nd Sts. • Subway: B, C to 72nd St.

Loeb Boathouse

The lake's eastern tip is graced by the elegant Loeb Boathouse. The large, copper-roofed, redbrick building opened in 1954, replacing a Victorian boathouse designed in 1874 by Calvert Vaux. You can rent bicycles to tour the park from here, and rowboats and Venetian gondolas (complete with singing gondoliers) to glide across the 18-acre (7.2 ha) lake, under the gaze of diners on the deck at the Boathouse Restaurant (see p. 126). For the city's bird-watchers, the boathouse is significant for a different reason, namely a communally written notebook detailing all bird sightings in the park, updated by enthusiasts almost every day. If you're an avid ornithologist, peruse the notebook and record your observations.

East side between 74th and 75th Sts. • www.thecentralparkboathouse.com • 212/517-2233 • Rowboat rentals: $$$ • Free Boathouse Restaurant trolley car departs from Fifth Ave. and 72nd St. every 20 minutes • Subway: 6 to 68th St.

From the Boathouse Restaurant diners can see across the lake toward Bethesda Terrace.

Strawberry Fields

4 The memorial to musician and songwriter John Lennon is a 2.5-acre (1 ha), tear-shaped garden across the street from **The Dakota** building (see pp. 136–137), where Lennon and his wife, Yoko Ono, lived at the time of his murder in 1980. The couple often visited this peaceful stretch of the park, which today attracts thousands of fans on the anniversaries of Lennon's birth (October 9) and death (December 8), with many staying late into the night singing their favorite songs. A black and white mosaic on the ground with the word "Imagine" marks the heart of the memorial, and a nearby bronze plaque lists the 121 countries that have donated trees, plants, and stones to endorse the site as a garden of peace. Many fans leave flowers, candles, and other gifts in tribute to the legendary Beatle.

Central Park West, between 72nd and 73rd Sts.
• Subway: B, C to 72nd St.

GOOD **EATS**

■ **BOATHOUSE RESTAURANT**
Although the food is great, it's the open-air views across the lake that make this restaurant a favorite with New Yorkers.
Loeb Boathouse, East 72nd St. and Park Dr. North, 212/517-2233, $$$$$

■ **CAFÉ SABARSKY**
This Viennese standout in the Neue Galerie is known for its excellent goulash, sausages, strudels, and tortes.
1048 Fifth Ave. and 88th St., 212/288-0665, $$$

■ **CALLE OCHO**
Near Shakespeare Garden, try delicious Latino fare washed down with sangria in a glowing, friendly environment.
446 Columbus Ave., between 81st and 82nd Sts., 212/873-5025, $$$$$

Belvedere Castle

5 Standing at the highest point in the park, Belvedere Castle offers panoramic views of both greenery and cityscapes from its granite towers. When it was built in 1869, it was intended as a whimsical lookout. The National Weather Service has been taking the city's temperature from here every day since 1919. The castle also attracts nature enthusiasts: Borrow a **Discovery Kit** backpack containing binoculars, a guidebook, a map, and sketching materials for free, or enjoy events, including the **"On A Wing"** series, which explores Central Park's many winged creatures.

Mid-park at 79th St. • 212/772-0210 • Closed Mon.–Tues. Nov.–March and Mon. April–Oct. • Subway: B, C to 81st St.

CENTRAL PARK

Shakespeare Garden

6 Literature lovers should not miss Shakespeare Garden. The quiet, 4-acre (1.6 ha) spread abounds with many of the plants mentioned in Shakespeare's poems and plays, including the distinctly Elizabethan-sounding flax and cowslip, primrose, wormwood, quince, and lark's heel. Beautifully landscaped and secluded, with a twisting, ascending path dotted with rustic wooden benches and bronze plaques inscribed with quotations from the Bard, the garden is a hidden gem. Highlights include an enchanting stone staircase built into a steep slope, the **Swedish Cottage**— literally transported from Sweden in 1877 and now home to a marionette theater—and a mulberry tree that some believe was grown from a cutting taken in Shakespeare's mother's garden in Stratford-upon-Avon, England. The garden is especially spectacular in spring, when crocuses, hyacinths, and roses are in bloom.

West side, between 79th and 80th Sts. • Subway: B, C to 72nd St.

Conservatory Garden

7 This 6-acre (2.4 ha) garden is a popular spot for weddings, thanks to its fairy-tale-like setting. It is composed of three distinct sections: Italian, French, and English. The central, Italian-style garden is a large lawn, bordered by two pink-and-white crabtree allées. The French-inspired garden is bursting with color when tulips bloom in spring and in fall when chrysanthemums put on their annual show. Circular pathways meander around the English-style garden, as magnolias and Japanese lilac trees perfume the air in spring and summer. Tours of the garden are offered at 11 a.m. on Saturday mornings from April to October.

During spring in the French-inspired garden, tulips bloom behind the Untermayer Fountain.

East side, between Fifth Ave. and 105th St. • Subway: 6 to 103rd St.

The City's the Star

New York's towering buildings, hectic streets, and colorful characters have inspired many filmmakers since the 1890s, with some of America's best-loved movies set here. More than 200 films feature scenes that have been set in Central Park alone, from the sinister assault on Dustin Hoffman and his girlfriend in *Marathon Man* to the task-force-type penguins digging a tunnel to escape from the Central Park Zoo in *Madagascar.*

Next Stop, Greenwich Village was among several movies to feature Caffe Reggio (above). Audrey Hepburn attracted large crowds while filming the opening shots of *Breakfast at Tiffany's* (right).

Early Days

Although New York was first captured on the silver screen in William Heise's motion picture *Herald Square* (1896), many subsequent movies set in Manhattan were shot on California sets—such as Alfred Hitchcock's *Rear Window* in 1954. This changed with the 1960s "New Hollywood" film era, when filmmakers such as Martin Scorsese, Francis Ford Coppola, and Woody Allen created commercial and critical success with stories revolving around, and shot in, New York.

Downtown Realism

New York's Lower East Side is one of the city's oldest neighborhoods, with a rich history of immigrant culture. Coppola and Gordon Parks found inspiration here, though Greenwich Village's **Caffe Reggio** (see p. 65) appears as a backdrop in their gritty films, *The Godfather Part II* and *Shaft.* Farther south, **Little Italy**'s roads provided the ideal location for Scorsese's seedy, hard-hitting classics *Mean Streets* and *Taxi Driver.*

CENTRAL PARK

Uptown Charm

When Audrey Hepburn gazed into the window of **Tiffany & Co.,** she forever cemented Fifth Avenue's glamorous reputation. Farther up the avenue is the elegant **Plaza** hotel (see p. 183), home to Eloise from the eponymous children's books and movie, and the spot where a fictional young guest played by Macaulay Culkin racked up a thousand-dollar room service bill in *Home Alone II.*

Love is in the Air

Numerous sites feature in the city's romances. Rising above them all is the **Empire State Building** (see p. 78), scene of the emotional climaxes that brought *Sleepless in Seattle* and *An Affair to Remember* to a memorable close.

TV **TOURS**

Follow in the footsteps of your favorite TV characters on a guided tour based on famous shows. You'll visit spots such as the apartment building used in *Friends,* Aidan's Scout Bar from *Sex and the City, Gossip Girl*'s school and, of course, *The Sopranos'* Bada Bing nightclub. While on these tours you can eat, drink, and shop just like your favorite stars.

www.screentours.com, 212/683-2027, $$$$

CENTRAL PARK

Outdoor Activities

New York may be a concrete jungle, but there is plenty to do in the great outdoors. Join the cyclists and runners on the city's many miles of greenway. Take a relaxing summer swim in an outdoor pool, and you can even kayak on the Hudson River and get a fresh angle on the city experience.

■ BIKING

New York City opened the country's first bike path in 1894 and now has more than 250 miles (402 km) of cycling paths, many of them in Central Park. **Bike and Roll** has rental shops at various locations (*www.bikeand roll.com, 212/260-0400, closed Jan., Feb., and Dec., $$$*). The **Manhattan Waterfront Greenway,** which circumnavigates the island, is a 32-mile (51.5 km) traffic-free path for runners and cyclists. (To get there, ride west from Central Park directly to the Hudson River.) Most rentals include a helmet, basket, lock, and map. Stop for stop signs and red lights or face a fine.

Bike rentals are available at the Loeb Boathouse (see p. 125)

■ RUNNING

Central Park has lanes dedicated to running as well as biking. Every lamp post on the Central Park Loop—the 6-mile (9.6 km) interior road that encircles the park—is marked with a street number and a W (west) or E (east), so you cannot get lost easily. If you would prefer to run on the streets, keeping track of your mileage is easy: Every 20 blocks north-south is one mile (1.6 km). A memorable way to see Manhattan is from the waterfront, so try running along any stretch of the **Greenway**—most spots offer excellent views. You'll pass parks, harbors, and gardens, and see the **Statue of Liberty** (see pp. 50–51) and other city landmarks along the way.

www.centralparknyc.org

■ KAYAKING

The all-volunteer crew at the **New York City Downtown Boathouse** offers both formal kayaking lessons and less formal instruction in sit-on-top colorful plastic kayaks. It's perfect

It's polite to run counterclockwise around Central Park's lake.

for both children and beginners, who can safely play on the Hudson and explore the river. This is a must-do, especially with kids—best of all, it's free.

Downtown Boathouse has three locations: Pier 40 (West Houston St.), Pier 96 (W. 57th St.), and 72nd St. at the edge of Riverside Park • www.downtownboathouse.org • E-mail: info@downtownboathouse.org • Open weekends and holidays, May–Oct.

■ SWIMMING

Want to take a dip but have no time to go to the beach? New York City has plenty of outdoor public pools perfect for those scorching summer afternoons. Central Park's **Lasker Pool,** in the northeast corner at 106th Street, is free and lets you enjoy views of Manhattan's skyscrapers. If you don't want to go when the city's children are splashing around, aim for the lap swim Monday through Friday from 7 a.m to 8:30 a.m. and 7 p.m. to 8:30 p.m. Bring your own lock, towel, bathing cap, and other gear. **Hamilton Fish Park** on the Lower East Side *(Pitt St. and Houston St., 212/387-7687)* has an Olympic-size pool as well as a large wading pool. Also, **Riverbank Public Park** *(679 Riverside Dr. at West 145 St., 212/694-3600, $)* has an Olympic-size pool.

www.nycgovparks.org

Upper West Side

The Upper West Side lies between Central Park and Riverside Park, and it is bounded to the south by Columbus Circle and to the north by 110th Street. Within these confines lie some of the city's most gracious residences, including ornate 19th-century brownstones that are synonymous with New York and some of the city's first luxury apartment buildings. Stroll the tree-lined streets and enjoy the rich and varied architecture, shop for everything from designer clothes to housewares at the glossy, ultramodern Time Warner Center, view cultural art at the American Folk Art Museum, and seek out world-class performances of classical music and opera at Lincoln Center. An ideal entry point into the Upper West Side for families is the American Museum of Natural History, which offers interactive displays to stimulate budding naturalists and scientists. As a tonic after savoring the sights, take in Riverside Park, less well known than Central Park but offering just as much—with the added bonus of Hudson River views.

134 **Neighborhood Walk**

140 **In Depth: American Museum of Natural History**

142 **Distinctly New York: The Brownstone**

144 **Best Of: Gourmet Shops**

❶ **Tended terrace gardens brighten the front of an apartment building on the Upper West Side.**

Upper West Side

Fine architecture and two of the city's most prestigious museums come together in this well-tended corner of Manhattan.

1 American Museum of Natural History (see pp. 140–141) Take a close look at gigantic dinosaur skeletons, fascinating dioramas, displays on evolution and biodiversity, and the state-of-the-art Rose Center for Earth and Space. Walk down one block.

7 Riverside Park (see p. 139) This 330-acre (134 ha) scenic sliver, stretching from 59th Street to 158th Street along the Hudson River, has ample opportunities for recreation or quiet contemplation and incredible waterfront views of the southern end of Manhattan and New Jersey.

0 — 600 meters
0 — 600 yards

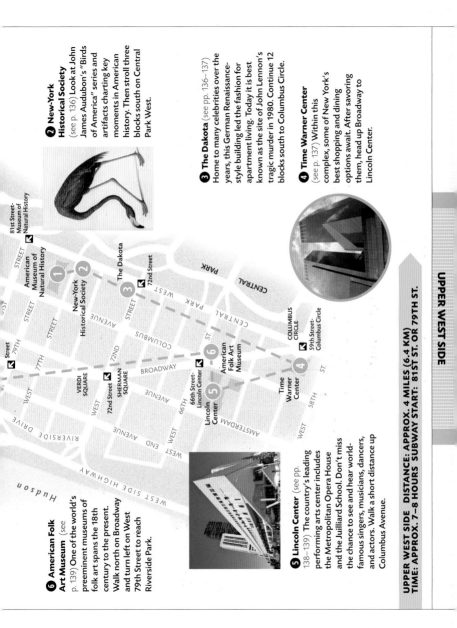

❷ New-York Historical Society

(see p. 136) Look at John James Audubon's "Birds of America" series and artifacts charting key moments in American history. Then stroll three blocks south on Central Park West.

❸ The Dakota (see pp. 136–137)

Home to many celebrities over the years, this German Renaissance-style building led the fashion for apartment living. Today it is best known as the site of John Lennon's tragic murder in 1980. Continue 12 blocks south to Columbus Circle.

❹ Time Warner Center

(see p. 137) Within this complex, some of New York's best shopping and dining options await. After savoring them, head up Broadway to Lincoln Center.

❻ American Folk Art Museum (see

p. 139) One of the world's preeminent museums of folk art spans the 18th century to the present. Walk north on Broadway and turn left on West 79th Street to reach Riverside Park.

❺ Lincoln Center (see pp.

138–139) The country's leading performing arts center includes the Metropolitan Opera House and the Juilliard School. Don't miss the chance to see and hear world-famous singers, musicians, dancers, and actors. Walk a short distance up Columbus Avenue.

UPPER WEST SIDE

UPPER WEST SIDE DISTANCE: APPROX. 4 MILES (6.4 KM)
TIME: APPROX. 7–8 HOURS SUBWAY START: 81ST ST. OR 79TH ST.

American Museum of Natural History

1 See pp. 140–141.

Central Park West at 79th St. • www.amnh.org • 212/769-5100 • $$$ • Closed Thanksgiving and Dec. 25 • Subway: B, C to 81st St.–Museum of Natural History

New-York Historical Society

2 Founded in 1804, the city's oldest museum, the New-York Historical Society, presents a compelling look back at the history of the United States through the lens of New York. (Even the hyphen in the museum's name, a convention used until the 1840s, is a history lesson.) The newly renovated galleries (opened in November 2011) display selections from 60,000 artifacts and works of art spanning four centuries, including an important **Tiffany lamp collection** and the complete **Birds of America** series, 435 watercolors by America's preeminent 19th-century wildlife artist, John James Audubon. Visitors can also peruse the research library on the second floor. Among its two million documents are dozens of standouts, including Napoleon's authorization for the **Louisiana Purchase** in 1803 and General Grant's handwritten terms of surrender to General Lee in 1865. The **Henry Luce Center** displays the museum's most prized pieces, such as a silk-upholstered chair that belonged to executed French queen Marie Antoinette.

170 Central Park West at 77th St. • www.nyhistory.org • 212/873-3400 • $$$ • Closed Mon., Thanksgiving, May 31, Dec. 25 • Subway: B, C to 81st St.–Museum of Natural History

Delicate "Dragonflies" is one of the lamps by Tiffany Studios at the New-York Historical Society.

The Dakota

3 The city's most famous apartment building is notable for its ornate features as well as its roster of past and present celebrity residents. When the building, designed by Henry J. Hardenbergh, was completed in 1884, the Upper West Side was so desolate that the building was

UPPER WEST SIDE

named after the remote Dakota Territory. But the distinctive, nine-story German Renaissance-style structure, with its detailed stonework, reliefs, balconies, and gables, greatly helped to transform the neighborhood. Judy Garland and Leonard Bernstein are among the Dakota's former residents, and, renamed The Bramford, it was the film home of Rosemary and John Woodhouse (Mia Farrow and John Cassavetes) in the 1968 horror classic *Rosemary's Baby*. Though designated a National Historic Landmark in 1976, it is almost impossible to step inside one of the Dakota's luxurious apartments: The residents are fiercely protective of their privacy, and a taciturn doorman guards the building's entrance at all hours.

1 West 72nd St. • Subway: B, C to 72nd St.

Time Warner Center

4 The gleaming complex rising out of Columbus Circle has some of the city's best shopping, dining, entertainment, and accommodations. The center contains more than 40 shops, from the cutting edge (Montmartre and denim purveyor True Religion) to crowd pleasers (J. Crew and Williams-Sonoma), and several high-end restaurants. Rotating art exhibits enliven the lobbies, and **Jazz at Lincoln Center** (*www.jalc.org, 212/258-9800*) runs a program of world-class live jazz concerts from several venues in the complex, including the late-night **Dizzy's Club *Coca-Cola*.** Visit the stylish Mandarin Oriental hotel, on the 35th to 54th floors, for its superb views of Central Park and beyond.

10 Columbus Circle • www.shopsatcolumbuscircle.com • 212/823-6300
• Subway: 1, A, B, C, D to 59th St.–Columbus Circle

GOOD **EATS**

■ A VOCE COLUMBUS
In a handsomely designed space, friendly staff serve regional Italian specialties. **3rd floor, Time Warner Center, 212/823-2523, $$$$**

■ MASA
One of few NYC restaurants to be awarded three Michelin stars, the Shinto-like Masa, helmed by chef Masa Takayama, offers imaginative dishes. **4th floor, Time Warner Center, 212/823-9800, $$$$$**

■ PER SE
At Thomas Keller's world-famous restaurant expect the unforgettable—superb ingredients, perfect service, and a huge bill. Reservations required. **4th floor, Time Warner Center, 212/823-9335, $$$$$**

■ WHOLE FOODS
Take your pick from a sushi bar, pizza station, and more, and nosh in the store's crowded but pleasant café. **Lower level, Time Warner Center, $**

Lincoln Center

5 Comprising 12 arts organizations, the Lincoln Center for the Performing Arts includes the **Metropolitan Opera,** the **New York City Ballet,** and the **New York Philharmonic.** A $1.2-billion renovation, which was launched shortly before Lincoln Center's 50th anniversary in 2009, has expanded and revitalized a number of buildings, including **Alice Tully Hall,** where the Chamber Society performs. Among the most spectacular venues is the **Metropolitan Opera House,** a colossal building with a gorgeous interior complete with a 24-carat gold leaf ceiling and a grand, spiraling staircase. All the world's greatest opera singers have performed here, including Luciano Pavarotti, Enrico Caruso, and Maria Callas. Though most performances command top prices, a new program offers discounted day-of tickets at the David Rubenstein Atrium *(Broadway at 62nd St., 212/875-5456),* so it's now easier to snag coveted seats. But there are plenty of ways to enjoy Lincoln Center for no money at

A lighted fountain splashes in front of the Metropolitan Opera House at Lincoln Center.

all—the expansive plazas are great spots for strolling, and there are scores of free happenings, like the family-focused "Meet the Artist" Saturdays series, which features acts such as hip-hop Shakespeare.

Between West 62nd and 65th Sts., and Columbus and Amsterdam Aves. • www .lincolncenter.org • 212/546-2656 • Subway: 1 to 66th St.–Lincoln Center

American Folk Art Museum

From handmade quilts and weathervanes to cookie jars and hunting decoys, this museum collects and displays folk art of the 18th and 19th centuries. While American art remains the main focus, the museum has expanded its vision to include European and Latin American pieces as well. Works by self-taught contemporary artists, such as Henry Darger, are another specialty. The museum recently moved from its site alongside MoMA to the space opposite Lincoln Center, where it has staged exhibitions since 1989.

2 Lincoln Square • www.folkartmuseum.org • 212/595-9533 • $$$ • Closed Mon., Jan. 1, July 4, Thanksgiving, Dec. 25 • Subway: 1 to 66th St.–Lincoln Center

Riverside Park

Created by Frederick Law Olmsted, co-designer of Central Park, Riverside Park is much prized by local residents for its tranquility and superb facilities. Begin exploring at 70th Street, where you can also rent bicycles. **Pier 1** at 70th Street is an ideal spot for fishing and relaxing, and a summer venue for free events such as concerts and kids' shows. At the 79th Street **Boat Basin** you can glimpse yachts and sailboats, or grab a snack at the **Boat Basin Café.** Of the park's 15 playgrounds, the **River Run Playground** *(82nd St.)*, with its miniature Hudson River, is one of the best. From 83rd Street, the half-mile (0.8 km) **Serpentine Promenade,** a bike and running path, snakes past the **Soldiers' and Sailors' Memorial** to New Yorkers who died in the Civil War and the **91st Street Garden**, its lovely flowerbeds tended by die-hard volunteers.

Riverside Dr. at West 96th St. • www.nycgovparks.org • Subway: 1, 2, 3 to 72nd St.

American Museum of Natural History

Gain insights into life on Earth and enjoy virtual travel in space.

"The Spectrum of Life" exhibit displays thousands of specimens, from bacteria to mammals.

With its darkened galleries packed with eerily realistic dioramas and massive dinosaur skeletons, it's little wonder that kids and adults alike find this a magical place. The nearly 150-year-old institution occupies four blocks and is one of the world's most important scientific museums. Besides the memorable permanent displays, six groundbreaking exhibits are always on rotation, a Discovery Room provides kids with hands-on activities, and the renovated IMAX theater shows movies every hour.

MILSTEIN HALL OF OCEAN LIFE

A 94-foot-long (28.6 m) **model of a blue whale** hangs from the ceiling in this recently redesigned hall on the first floor. High-definition video projections, interactive computer stations, and models of more than 750 sea creatures, from microscopic algae to glowing jellyfishes, all combine to immerse visitors in life under the sea.

HALL OF BIODIVERSITY

Also on the first floor, this hall attracts visitors to see the psychedelic installation of specimens titled "**The Spectrum of Life.**" Even more spectacular, the interactive **rain-forest diorama** combines video, sound, and smell to simulate the experience of stepping into a rain forest. The display stresses the need to preserve the variety and interdependence of Earth's life-forms.

MARGARET MEAD HALL OF PACIFIC PEOPLES

This third-floor hall features the studies of the famous anthropologist Margaret Mead (1901–1978), who worked in the museum's Anthropology Department for

most of her life. The exhibition focuses on the myriad cultures of the South Pacific islands, including Polynesia and Micronesia. A group of traditional masks made of wood and bark from Papua New Guinea ranks top among its highlights.

ROSE CENTER FOR EARTH AND SPACE

On ground level on the museum's north side, you will find the most exciting recent addition to the museum—the ultramodern Rose Center, a giant glass cube enveloping the Hayden Planetarium. Experience a virtual journey through space via a uniquely powerful **reality simulator,** and witness the beginnings of the universe in the **Big Bang.** Other standouts include the **Hall of Planet Earth** and the **Cosmic Pathway** that charts 13 billion years of evolution.

UPPER WEST SIDE

Central Park West at 79th St. • www.amnh.org • 212/769-5100 • $$$ • Closed Thanksgiving and Dec. 25 • Subway: B, C to 81st St.–Museum of Natural History

The Brownstone

No residential building in New York City is more iconic than the aptly named brownstone; long rows of these narrow, three-to-six-story homes distinguish neighborhoods on the Upper West Side and elsewhere in Manhattan and Brooklyn. They often serve as fictional residences in movies and television series—for example, the characters in Spike Lee's films habitually pass the time on the stoops of brownstones in Brooklyn.

Carved stone foliage detailing is a feature of the brownstone (above). Classic row houses fan out along Berkeley Place, Brooklyn (right).

Desirable Residences

In New York, the term "brownstone" refers to any kind of row house, whether of brick, limestone, or marble. Some of the city's first row houses started popping up in the late 18th century in lower Manhattan and were characterized by their colonial design, small size, and brick exterior. Beginning in the 1850s, brownstone, quarried in Connecticut and New Jersey, became the building material of choice. Everyone from middle-class families to the city's elite aspired to live in a brownstone, including the railroad magnate William H. Vanderbilt, who owned a $2 million pair at 640 and 642 Fifth Avenue.

Features that were subsequently added are now considered quintessential characteristics, such as a steeply sloped stoop and decorative molding around the windows and doors. By the late 1870s, much of the city was filled with densely packed brownstones, but the Upper West Side remained largely undeveloped. The introduction of an elevated train to the neighborhood in 1879 kicked off a period of huge growth. The architectural styles of this era, including Queen Anne, Romanesque, and Renaissance Revival, encouraged unusual artistic freedom and eclecticism. On the Upper West Side, the houses were visually distinct from one another, often with different colored bricks and stone on a single façade—much to the taste of their socially competitive residents.

Return to Glory

Since the 1960s, many of these buildings have been restored to their original grandeur. The Upper West Side, Chelsea, Greenwich Village, and parts of Brooklyn (see pp. 162–163) are now being celebrated for their streets of majestic row houses.

see pp. 162–163

DON'T **MISS**

73rd Street, between Central Park West and Columbus Avenue—Queen Anne-style brownstones

East side of West End Avenue, between West 76th and West 77th Streets—an entire block of 1880s–1890s row houses

St. Luke's Place, between Seventh Avenue and Hudson Street—stunning 1850s Italianate row houses

Willow Street, between Pineapple and Clark Streets, Brooklyn—rare brownstone-front Gothic Revival row houses, at Nos. 118, 120, and 122

UPPER WEST SIDE

Gourmet Shops

On the Upper West Side and beyond, you don't have to go far to discover a gourmet food shop. Whether it's an old-school mom-and-pop establishment selling classic Italian imports or a new mega-store with several specialty stores under one roof, there's plenty to entice foodies to the Big Apple.

■ CITARELLA

One of the city's oldest specialty markets, Citarella began as a simple seafood market in Harlem in 1912. Owner Mike Citarella moved the flagship store to the Upper West Side, but his focus on quality fish didn't change. Today, at all five Citarella stores across the city and its environs, you'll find a pristine seafood counter loaded with everything from New Zealand cockles to whole wild bass, plus a variety of delicious prepared dishes, an excellent meat counter, and hundreds of cheeses.

2135 Broadway at 75th St. • www.citarella.com
• 212/874-0383

■ ZABAR'S

A few blocks away from Citarella on the Upper West Side, Zabar's is a beloved, family-owned delicatessen dating back to 1934 that has managed to retain its Old World charm. This is the place for smoked salmon and seafood salads, dozens of types of coffee, and delectable baked goods, like hearty rye bread and chocolate rugelach. The second floor is crammed with housewares worthy of lugging home. The store's adjoining café, which is usually packed with elderly neighborhood regulars, is a great spot for a bowl of matzo ball soup and a dense, onion knish.

2245 Broadway, between 80th and 81st Sts.
• www.zabars.com • 212/496-1234

■ DI PALO'S FINE FOODS

In Little Italy, the owners of Di Palo's Fine Foods take cheesemaking very seriously. Every day, Lou Di Palo, along with his brother and son, roll up their sleeves to make a batch of fresh mozzarella and ricotta, among other cheeses, following the same family recipe used since the store first opened in 1925. Di Palo's also sells an impressive array of imported Italian goods, such as prosciutto from

UPPER WEST SIDE

Russ & Daughters has been selling top-quality smoked fish and caviar since 1914.

Parma and speck (smoked, cured ham), from Alto Adige, as well as sweets, wine, and spirits from all over the country.

200 Grand St. between Mulberry and Mott Sts. • www.dipaloselects.com • 212/226-1033

■ DESPAÑA

This sleek SoHo shop, opened in 2006, has become the city's source for everything Spanish, from hand-sliced Ibérico ham and chorizo to paella pans and earthenware dishes called *cazuelas*. A café within the store serves excellent coffee, sandwiches, and typical tapas.

480 Broome St. at Cleveland Pl. • www.despananyc.com • 212/219-5050

■ RUSS & DAUGHTERS

This family-run shop reminiscent of an earlier era is a rarity. At the turn of the 20th century, when the Lower East Side was home to nearly two million Eastern European Jewish immigrants, appetizing stores—shops that, in accordance with kosher dietry laws, sold fish and dairy products but no meat—were commonplace. Today, Russ & Daughters is one of the few such stores to survive. It is one of the best places for cream cheese or lox bagels and fresh orange juice.

179 East Houston St., bet. Allen and Orchard Sts. • www.russanddaughters.com • 212/475-4880

The Heights & Harlem

Harlem runs the width of Manhattan from 96th Street on the south to 170th Street on the north. Until the 1970s and '80s, it was largely seen as a place to avoid, but restored brownstones, new galleries, and still thriving music venues have since made it a key part of the New York experience. African Americans flocked to the area in the early 20th century, when writers, intellectuals, and artists produced the phenomenon known as the Harlem Renaissance. El Barrio, in the southeast section, is home to a large Latino community, celebrated at the El Barrio museum. Washington Heights, named for George Washington, who fought there during the Revolutionary War, offers a little piece of medieval Europe in America—The Cloisters, an outpost of the Metropolitan Museum of Art.

148 **Neighborhood Walk**

154 **In Depth: The Cloisters**

156 **Distinctly New York: Harlem Renaissance**

◀ **The mural "How Do I See Myself?" shows self-portraits by local young artists and is one of several such artworks enlivening Harlem's streets.**

The Heights & Harlem

Multicultural arts and heritage beckon in Manhattan's northernmost neighborhoods.

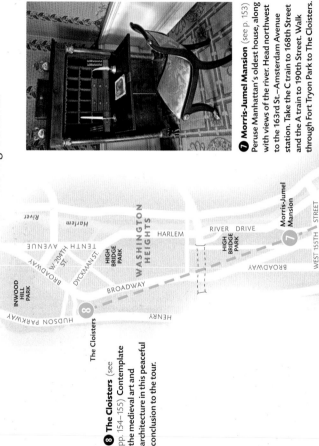

❼ Morris-Jumel Mansion (see p. 153) Peruse Manhattan's oldest house, along with views of the river. Head northwest to the 163rd St.–Amsterdam Avenue station. Take the C train to 168th Street and the A train to 190th Street. Walk through Fort Tryon Park to The Cloisters.

❽ The Cloisters (see pp. 154–155) Contemplate the medieval art and architecture in this peaceful conclusion to the tour.

INWOOD HILL PARK

HUDSON PARKWAY

BROADWAY

W. 204TH ST.

DYCKMAN ST.

TENTH AVENUE

Harlem River

HIGH BRIDGE PARK

WASHINGTON HEIGHTS

BROADWAY

HENRY

HARLEM

RIVER DRIVE

HIGH BRIDGE PARK

BROADWAY

WEST 155TH STREET

JACKIE

Morris-Jumel Mansion

The Cloisters

1 mile
1 kilometer

1 El Museo del Barrio (see p. 150) Begin by visiting New York's leading Latino cultural center. Go north up Fifth Avenue, then turn left along 110th Street and right on Amsterdam Avenue.

2 The Cathedral Church of St. John the Divine (see p. 151) The ethos of this great cathedral reflects local diversity and inclusiveness. Head west to Riverside Park.

3 General Grant National Memorial (see p. 151) The 18th president and the Union's most celebrated general of the Civil War, Grant is entombed at this mausoleum in Riverside Park. Zigzag east to West 125th Street.

4 Apollo Theater (see p. 152) This venue has launched the careers of many superstars. Continue west along West 125th Street.

5 The Studio Museum in Harlem (see p. 152) The first U.S. museum dedicated to black artists features African-American art from the 19th and 20th centuries. Head north to Adam C. Powell Boulevard, and turn right on 138th Street.

6 The Abyssinian Baptist Church (see p. 153) Harlem's most prominent church has a famed gospel choir. From Adam C. Powell Boulevard, take the M2 bus north to West 160th Street and walk west to Jumel Terrace.

THE HEIGHTS & HARLEM   DISTANCE: APPROX. 8 MILES (13 KM)
TIME: 8 HOURS   SUBWAY START: 103RD STREET

El Museo del Barrio

1 This museum in East (Spanish) Harlem, or El Barrio, at the top end of Fifth Avenue's Museum Mile, started life modestly in 1969 as a place to curate and display the art and history of New York's Puerto Rican community. Today, the museum's collection of more than 6,500 paintings, sculptures, photographs, and other works of art spans at least 800 years of Latino, Latin American, and Caribbean culture, from pre-Columbian Taíno artifacts to late 20th-century pieces. Highlights of the museum include "The All-Powerful Hand of Christ (La Mano Poderosa)" by Puerto Rican artist Norberto Cedeño, and a stone **Taíno ceremonial belt** (1200–1500). Signage on the exhibits is in both English and Spanish.

1230 Fifth Ave. at 104th St. • www.elmuseo.org • 212/831-7272 • $$ • Closed Mon., Jan. 1, July 4, Thanksgiving, Dec. 25 • Subway: 6 to 103rd St. or 2, 3 to 110th St.

"La Cama" by Puerto Rican artist Pepón Osorio forms part of El Museo del Barrio's collection.

The Cathedral Church of St. John the Divine

One of the world's largest cathedrals has a floor area of 121,000 square feet (11,240 sq m) and a 232-foot-high (71 m) vault. Built in fits and starts beginning in 1892, in a mixture of Gothic, Romanesque, and Byzantine styles, it is still only two-thirds complete and popularly known as St. John the Unfinished. One incomplete arch, known as **Pearl Harbor Arch,** has been left in memory of a stonecarver who never returned from World War II. The cathedral's seven **Chapels of the Tongues,** each one dedicated to a different immigrant group, reflect New York City's diversity. All are welcome here, including four-legged creatures—the annual Blessing of the Animals in October has included a tortoise, a macaw, and a yak. The grounds have a children's sculpture garden, ecology trail, and Peace Fountain. On Saturdays at noon and 2 p.m., you can climb 124 feet (38 m) up spiral staircases to the top of the cathedral to study the architecture and stained-glass windows.

1047 Amsterdam Ave. at West 112th St. • www.stjohndivine.org • 212/316-7540 • $ (donation) • Subway: 1 to Cathedral Parkway

General Grant National Memorial

A grand, granite mausoleum overlooking the Hudson River in the north of Riverside Park (see p. 139) is the final resting place of President Ulysses S. Grant and his wife, Julia. The tomb—the largest in North America—was completed in 1897 and is engraved with the words "Let us have peace," a line from Grant's speech to the 1868 Republican Convention that became his slogan in the subsequent presidential campaign. When the former Civil War general died in 1885, around 90,000 people donated more than $600,000 to build his tomb—then the largest public fundraising effort in U.S. history. Until World War II, it was a more popular attraction than the Statue of Liberty. During the summer, there are outdoor concerts and a ranger-led walk through Riverside Park.

Riverside Dr. at West 122nd St. • www.nps.gov/gegr • 212/666-1640 • Closed Jan. 1, Thanksgiving, Dec. 25 • Subway: 1 to 125th St.

"Amateur Night" at the Apollo teams up would-be stars with vociferous audiences who revel in the party-like atmosphere.

Apollo Theater

④ This legendary theater, built in 1914, launched the careers of many great performers—including Jimi Hendrix, Gladys Knight, the Jackson Five, and Diana Ross. Most emerging stars got their break by winning "Amateur Night," Ella Fitzgerald being the first to do so in 1934. Since then audiences have been cheering and jeering performers every Wednesday night beginning at 7:30 p.m. You too can join in encouraging (or not) new talent as a succession of singers, dancers, guitarists, and other artists bravely takes the stage. The Apollo also hosts top acts, such as Stevie Wonder and Salif Keita, in addition to fresh talent.

253 West 125th St. between Seventh and Eighth Aves.
• www.apollotheater.org • 212/531-5300 • Amateur Night: $$$$ • Subway: 2, 3, A, B, C, D to 125th St.

The Studio Museum in Harlem

⑤ Founded in 1968, the first U.S. art museum dedicated to black artists houses 19th- and 20th-century African-American paintings and sculptures, as well as work by artists from elsewhere in the African diaspora. The permanent collection includes photographs by Dawoud Bey and paintings by Jacob Lawrence and Alma Thomas, but the crown jewels are the photographs by James VanDerZee. From the early 1900s until his death in 1983, VanDerZee chronicled the lives of the people of Harlem, including black nationalist leader Marcus Garvey and poet Countee Cullen. His shots of jazz clubs and restaurants in the 1920s and '30s capture the vibrant spirit of the neighborhood.

144 West 125th St. between Seventh Ave. and Malcolm X Blvd.
• www.studiomuseum.org • 212/864-4500 • $$ • Closed: Mon., Tues., Wed., and major public holidays • Subway: 2, 3, A, B, C, D to 125th St.

THE HEIGHTS & HARLEM

The Abyssinian Baptist Church

6 New York's first African-American Baptist church offers the chance to listen to one of the nation's finest gospel choirs. Founded in 1808 by a group of African Americans and Ethiopian sea merchants, Harlem's most prominent church has more than 4,000 parishioners. If you wish to attend the 11 a.m. Sunday service, get there early; parishioners get first dibs on the church's 1,000-odd seats, and the visitors' line typically stretches around the block. Be sure to dress appropriately—no tank tops, shorts, or flip-flops; and remember that you are asked to stay for the full two-and-a-half-hour service.

132 Odell Clark Pl. at Seventh Ave. • www.abyssinian.org • 212/862-7474 • Subway: 2, 3, A, B, C to 135th St.

Morris-Jumel Mansion

7 Built in 1765, this Georgian-style mansion served as home and battle headquarters to George Washington in 1776. Located on a hilltop overlooking the Hudson River, it gave Washington a strategic advantage in the Battle of Harlem Heights against the British. Inside the house, which is Manhattan's oldest personal residence, each room is decorated to re-create a part of its history, including the colonial period, the Revolutionary War, and the new republic.

65 Jumel Ter. • www.morrisjumel.org • 212/923-8008 • $ • Closed Mon., Tues., Jan. 1, Thanksgiving, Dec. 25, and major public holidays • Subway: 2, 3, A, B, C to 135th St.

The Cloisters

8 See pp. 154–155.

99 Margaret Corbin Dr. • www.metmuseum .org/cloisters • 212/923-3700 • $$$$ • Closed Mon., Jan. 1, Thanksgiving, Dec. 25 • Subway: C to 168th St. or A to 190th St.

GOOD **EATS**

■ **NEW LEAF RESTAURANT**
This restaurant, housed in a 1930s cobblestone building in Fort Tryon Park a short walk from The Cloisters (see pp. 154–155), is an escape from the city's hustle and bustle. It's run by the New York Restoration Project, a nonprofit that helps to improve city parks. **1 Margaret Corbin Dr., 212/568-5323, $$$$**

■ **RED ROOSTER**
Cookbook writer and chef Marcus Samuelsson's new restaurant serves Southern comfort food, including blackened catfish and black-eyed peas. **310 Lenox Ave., between 125th and 126th Sts., 212/792-9001, $$$**

■ **SYLVIA'S RESTAURANT**
Head to this legendary spot for Sunday brunch, where you can listen to gospel music and feast on soul food. Since Sylvia Woods opened this restaurant in 1962, it's become a hot spot for residents and tourists alike. **328 Lenox Ave. at West 127th St., 212/996-0660, $$**

The Cloisters

*Wander among some of the world's greatest medieval artworks
in a tranquil setting reminiscent of early monastic life.*

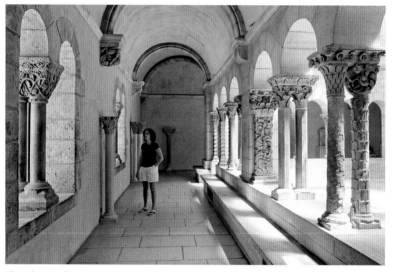

The columns of Saint-Guilhem-le-Désert (circa 1206) display a wealth of carved detail.

The remains of five French cloisters and other religious sites were shipped
from Europe in the early 20th century by an American collector and bought
by the Metropolitan Museum of Art in 1925, and added to subsequently. The
Cloisters' collection of medieval European art and architecture—around 3,000
pieces from the ninth to the 16th centuries—is arranged in chronological
order. Set above the Hudson River in Upper Manhattan's Fort Tryon Park, the
whole site is invitingly small, and its displays can be viewed in a single visit.

■ EARLY MEDIEVAL MASTERPIECES

Downstairs in the Treasury, the "**Cloisters Cross**" is an intricate Romanesque altar cross made of walrus tusk, with immense visual and spiritual appeal. Although less than two feet (0.6 m) high, it is meticulously carved with 92 tiny figures and 98 inscriptions on the front and back. It is sometimes called the Bury St. Edmunds Cross, for the monastery in England where it may have originated.

Among the architectural stars are early **13th-century columns and pilasters** that are part of the Saint-Guilhem Cloister—originally from the Benedictine Abbey of Saint-Guilhem-le-Désert near Montpellier, France. The decoration includes acanthus leaf and blossom designs, while some of the capitals have a lacy effect created by skillful drilling.

■ TEXTILES & FINE ART

The stunning "**Unicorn Tapestries**," in an eponymous room, depict the dramatic hunt and capture of a unicorn. These seven fantastical 15th-century wall hangings were probably commissioned by Anne of Brittany, the richest woman in Europe, to celebrate her marriage to King Louis XII of France. Beautifully preserved, the tapestries still glisten with strands of gold and silver.

In the Campin Room, a jewel-toned triptych known as the "**Merode Altarpiece**" (circa 1425), attributed to Robert Campin, depicts the Annunciation. It also shows Joseph busy in his workshop, having just made two mousetraps, and details of everyday life in a Flemish town.

■ THE GARDENS

The Cloisters' **enclosed gardens** are designed and maintained to emulate a medieval original in layout and horticulture, based on evidence from primary sources. As well as being educational, they are a great place to relax and spend a sunny day.

SAVVY **TRAVELER**

Tours of the collection highlights take place every afternoon except Saturday. Also, from May through October daily, experts in horticulture and tree husbandry conduct lunchtime tours of the gardens. Neither tour requires extra fees or reservations.

99 Margaret Corbin Dr., Fort Tryon Park • www.metmuseum.org/cloisters • 212/923-3700 • $$$$ • Closed Mon., Jan. 1, Thanksgiving, Dec. 25 • Subway: C to 168th St. or A to 190th St.

Harlem Renaissance

Though slavery ended in 1863, blacks, especially in the South, remained segregated from and mistreated by whites. So African Americans moved north to seek better lives. They settled in Harlem beginning around 1910, and over time many made their voices heard as poets, intellectuals, and musicians in what became known as the Harlem Renaissance. All took pride in their culture and believed they were forging a greater respect for their race.

The song "I'm Just Wild about Harry" (above) from the musical *Shuffle Along* became a huge hit. The Cotton Club's brilliant musicians attracted celebrity guests (right).

Cultural Blossoming

The migration of African Americans to northern cities—especially to Harlem—in the early 20th century created a vibrant atmosphere in which black writers began to articulate the experiences of black Americans.

One of the most successful authors of the period was Langston Hughes. With poems such as "The Negro Speaks of Rivers," he wrote about what it was like to be black in America and encouraged others to do the same. Zora Neale Hurston was the leading black female writer of the period, best known for *Their Eyes Were Watching God,* one of the first novels based on a black woman's voyage of self discovery. Both writers celebrated their blackness, rejecting the role of a second-class citizen.

In 1925, African-American professor Alain Locke edited a collection of poems and essays by black writers called *The New Negro.* The book shattered stereotypes, and it was key to defining the Harlem Renaissance. Locke wrote: "In the very process of being transplanted, the Negro is

THE HEIGHTS & HARLEM

becoming transformed…. In Harlem, Negro life is seizing upon its first chances for group expression and self-determination."

All That Jazz

Southern blacks brought new rhythms with them when they moved north. Jazz musicians and singers including Louis Armstrong, Bessie Smith, and Duke Ellington performed at clubs and theaters, some of which, such as the Cotton Club and the Roseland Ballroom, only served white patrons.

Black theater also had a renaissance. *Shuffle Along* became the first all African-American musical to play on Broadway—to a white audience—in 1921. The play had a sophisticated love story and led to more firsts for African Americans in the medium.

HARLEM **JAZZ**

Harlem honors its jazz culture with clubs and a museum:

American Legion Post 398 (see p. 69)

The Cotton Club The house band still performs great jazz music in an old-style location. **656 West 125th St. at Riverside Dr., www.cotton club-newyork.com, 212/663-7980**

Lenox Lounge (see p. 69)

The National Jazz Museum in Harlem Peruse a rich library on local jazz history. **104 East 126th St. at Park Ave., www .jazzmuseuminharlem.org, 212/348-8300**

BROOKLYN

Brooklyn

Artists from Walt Whitman to Spike Lee have drawn inspiration from dynamic Brooklyn. Settled by the Dutch in 1636 and named Breuckelen, it was an independent city until 1898, when it was incorporated as a borough of New York. In the ensuing years, everyone from New England farmers to European immigrants put down roots in this rural swath of land, now occupying around 71 square miles (184 sq km). Brooklyn still attracts immigrants from all over the world, making it one of the most diverse boroughs in the United States and a great place to explore the cuisines and traditions of other cultures. What's more, Brooklyn no longer plays second best to Manhattan. Increasingly, artists, students, and Manhattan defectors are choosing to live in this less-expensive borough, and they have helped transform industrial areas into buzzing hipster enclaves. Elegant Brooklyn Heights and the world-class Brooklyn Museum, along with gorgeous gardens and arts centers, quirky boutiques and top musical venues, lie just a walk away across the East River.

BROOKLYN

160 **Neighborhood Walk**

168 **In Depth: Brooklyn Museum**

170 **Distinctly New York: Bridges**

172 **Best Of: Parks & Gardens**

◐ **Gracious brownstones typify the quiet streets of Brooklyn Heights.**

NEIGHBORHOOD **WALK**

BROOKLYN

❶ Brooklyn Bridge (see p. 162) Begin by crossing the country's most influential bridge, which inspired both architect Frank Lloyd Wright and artist Georgia O'Keeffe. Leave the bridge via Cadman Plaza West/ Old Fulton Street. Walk down Middagh Street to Willow Street.

❷ Brooklyn Heights' Historic Houses (see pp. 162–163) Charming Willow Street has some of the city's best-preserved architecture. After exploring, follow Middagh Street to Columbia Heights.

❸ Brooklyn Heights Promenade (see pp. 163–164)
This scenic stretch, with views across the harbor to Lower Manhattan, is ideal for strolling and photography. Take the 2 train from Clark Street to Eastern Parkway–Brooklyn Museum.

**BROOKLYN   DISTANCE: APPROX. 7 MILES (11 KM)
TIME: 7–10 HOURS   SUBWAY START: BROOKLYN BRIDGE–CITY HALL**

Brooklyn

New York's most populous borough balances tranquil green spaces and historic architecture with a thriving arts scene.

4 Brooklyn Museum (see pp. 168–169) One of the country's oldest and largest art museums houses an Egyptian collection and a center devoted to feminist art. Walk east down Eastern Parkway.

5 Brooklyn Botanic Garden (see pp. 164–165) A series of gardens-within-a-garden, this peaceful area provides delight to the horticulturist and relaxation for all. Walk northwest along Eastern Parkway to Grand Army Plaza.

6 Central Library (see p. 165) The majestic flagship of the country's fifth largest library system has rare collections and hosts regular readings, concerts, and other events. Enter Prospect Park by its main entrance in the heart of Grand Army Plaza.

7 Prospect Park (see p. 166) Lose yourself in the borough's only forest, look for rare birds, or take advantage of the park's cultural offerings. Leave the park at Plaza Street West, and then walk up Union Street to Seventh Avenue.

8 Park Slope (see pp. 166–167) For eating and shopping, you'll find yourself spoiled for choice in and around Fifth and Seventh Avenues in this sought-after neighborhood.

Brooklyn Bridge

One of the engineering marvels of the 19th century, the world's first steel suspension bridge, completed in 1883, overawed onlookers with its size (see p. 170). Awe-inspiring it was, but also serviceable: In 1884, circus-founder P. T. Barnum paraded over it with 21 elephants to demonstrate its safety. Today, whether you walk, run, skate, or bike over it, crossing the Brooklyn Bridge is a must for any visitor to New York City. Unparalleled views of Manhattan, the East River, and the Statue of Liberty unfold before your eyes, along with an up-close look at the bridge's massive, neo-Gothic towers and criss-crossing wire cables, inviting myriad photo opportunities. Starting in Manhattan's Financial District, a walk across the 6,000-foot-long (1,830 m) bridge takes about 45 minutes. Pedestrians use an elevated footpath separated from the traffic below.

Access the bridge at Park Row and Centre St., Manhattan • www.visitbrooklyn.org • 718/802-3820 • Subway: 4, 5, 6 to Brooklyn Bridge–City Hall • Exit at Tillary and Adams Sts. or Prospect St., Brooklyn

Brooklyn Heights' Historic Houses

Few New York neighborhoods rival Brooklyn Heights for its historic buildings. Some of the borough's first brick houses and brownstones (see pp. 142–143) were built here after 1814, when a regular ferry service between Manhattan and Brooklyn was established. Designated New York's first historic district in 1965, the neighborhood has since been protected from invasive development. A walk down **Willow Street** reveals some of the handsomest and most architecturally diverse buildings. Highlights include **Nos. 108, 110,** and **112,** three Queen Anne–style row houses built in 1880; and **Nos. 155, 157,** and **159,** redbrick, Federal-style homes from 1826 that have their original doorways and ironwork. Other gems await on the streets that cross Willow—Cranberry, Orange, Pineapple, and Clark Streets. Three blocks south, **Our Lady of Lebanon Maronite Cathedral** (*113 Remsen St., www.ololc. org, 718/624-7228*), completed in 1846 by architect Richard

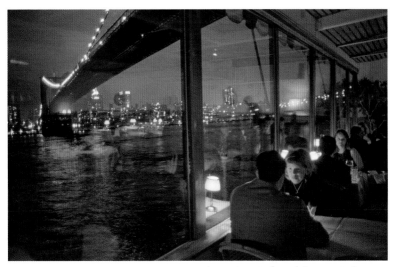

Under the Brooklyn Bridge, the River Café commands spectacular views of Lower Manhattan.

Upjohn, who designed Wall Street's Trinity Church (see p. 47), was the first Romanesque Revival-style building constructed in America. To soak up more of the borough's history, head back two blocks to the **Brooklyn Historical Society** *(221 Pierrepoint St., www.brooklynhistory .org, 718/222-4111, $$, closed Mon. and Tues.).* Carved figures decorate the terra-cotta Queen Anne building, designed by architect George B. Post in 1881. Inside, exhibits range from Brooklyn's beloved sports team, the Dodgers, to its long and illustrious history of beer brewing.

Willow St. runs between Middagh and Pierrepoint Sts. • Subway: 2, 3 to Clark St.

Brooklyn Heights Promenade

3 One of the most picturesque and romantic spots in the city, this promenade is perched high above the East River and the Brooklyn Queens Expressway (BQE), with lovely views of the harbor, Lower Manhattan, and the Brooklyn Bridge. Stretching for one-third of a mile

(0.5 km) between Remsen and Orange Streets, the parklike expanse draws everyone from tourists and old-timers, to teenage couples and families. Completed in 1950 under the influential city builder Robert Moses, the promenade was created, in part, to appease residents who opposed the construction of the BQE. The design works surprisingly well; even the noise of cars whizzing below is soothing, calling to mind rushing water more than traffic. Along the way, watch for a stone marking the land where George Washington's headquarters stood during the Revolutionary War, and a granite thunderbird honoring the Canarsie Indians who lived in the area.

Access the promenade from Middagh St.–Columbia Heights • www.nyharbor parks.org • 212/825-6880 • Subway: 2, 3 to Clark St.

Brooklyn Museum

4

See pp. 168–169.

200 Eastern Parkway • www.brooklynmuseum.org • 718/638-5000 • $$ • Closed Mon. and Tues. • Subway: 2,3 to Eastern Parkway–Brooklyn Museum

The Brooklyn Botanic Garden combines riotous flower plantings with a calming Japanese garden.

Brooklyn Botanic Garden

5

A horticultural triumph, the 52-acre (21 ha) Brooklyn Botanic Garden, adjacent to Prospect Park, has been one of the borough's great attractions since 1910. Immaculately maintained, the garden, which is home to wild rabbits, ducks, and turtles, seems instantly to induce a state of calm. Among its highlights are more than 200 cherry trees, which are covered in blooms in April. Set among rolling hills, the **Japanese Hill-and-Pond Garden** incorporates traditional elements such as a Shinto shrine by the pond, overhung with evergreen trees that make this a truly meditative spot. Other highlights include a **rose garden** with more than 1,400 varietals;

an outstanding **orchid collection,** including the giant species, *Grammatophyllum speciosum;* a **Discovery Garden** with hands-on activities for children; and a **Bonsai Museum** with 350 trees. Also interesting is a **Fragrance Garden** for the sight-impaired; created in 1955 and the first of its kind in the country, the area encourages visitors to smell and touch plants such as Corsican mint, Indian patchouli, and lavender. Don't miss the gallery on the lower level of the **Steinhardt Conservatory,** with a multimedia display about the natural world and sustainability, and installations by artists in residence.

900 Washington Ave. • www.bbg.org • 718/623-7200 • $$
• Closed Mon. and major holidays • Subway: B, Q to Prospect Park

Central Library

The crown jewel of the 60-branch Brooklyn Public Library system, the majestic Central Library is conveniently located just steps away from the Brooklyn Botanic Garden. Constructed in 1941 in contemporary art moderne style—a variant of art deco—the building resembles an open book, with the spine on Grand Army Plaza and the library's two wings opening like book covers along Eastern Parkway and Flatbush Avenue. The grand, recently redesigned entrance and plaza form a pleasant backdrop for a free summer concert series. The branch also hosts regular author talks, book discussions, and film screenings. The library houses the **Brooklyn Collection,** composed of historic photographs, drawings, memorabilia, and the complete archive of the *Brooklyn Eagle* newspaper (1841–1963). The poet and local resident Walt Whitman served as editor of the newspaper for two years.

10 Grand Army Plaza • www.brooklynpubliclibrary.org • 718/230-2100
• Subway: 2, 3 to Grand Army Plaza

GOOD **EATS**

■ **BROOKLYN ICE CREAM FACTORY**
Facing the East River in a historic fireboat house, the Brooklyn Ice Cream Factory sells delectable ice cream in eight classic flavors. **Corner of Old Fulton and Water Sts., 718/246-3963, $**

■ **GRIMALDI'S**
Just under the Brooklyn Bridge, Grimaldi's is a coal-brick-oven pizzeria. Despite the long line, you'll be seated in 30 minutes. **19 Old Fulton St., 718/858-4300, $$**

■ **RIVER CAFÉ**
On the waterfront with stunning views of Manhattan, the Michelin-starred River Café is a ravishing venue for brunch, lunch, or dinner, and it has produced some of the city's best chefs. **1 Water St., 718/522-5200, $$$$$**

BROOKLYN

Prospect Park

7 Central Park may be more famous, but Brooklynites are fiercely loyal to Prospect Park, a 585-acre (237 ha) sweep of woods, hills, lakes, and waterfalls. Constructed by Central Park's designers, Frederick Law Olmsted and Calvert Vaux, and opened in 1867, Prospect Park has opportunities to relax, go boating, enjoy live music, and cozy up to farm animals. The **Audubon Center** at the Boathouse (*Lincoln Road–Ocean Avenue entrance*), housed in a 1905 beaux arts building, contains an information center and kid-friendly exhibits. From here, scenic trails snake through the forest and pass by the 60-acre (24 ha) lake. Bird lovers will be delighted by the park's 200-species bird population, which includes green herons and red-tailed hawks. On Saturdays, a **farmer's market** (*Grand Army Plaza entrance*) overflows with produce. In summer, the **Bandshell** (*Prospect Park West and 9th Street*) hosts performances by world-famous artists, and the New York Philharmonic Orchestra offers free concerts on the **Long Meadow.** Check out the **Prospect Park Zoo** (*Lincoln Road–Ocean Avenue entrance*), with its collection of 400 animals; youngsters can feed the farm animals.

95 Prospect Park West • www.prospectpark.org • 718/965-8951 • Audubon Center: 718/287-3400 • Closed Mon.–Fri. Feb.–March; Mon.–Wed. April–Sept. except public holidays; and Oct.–Jan. • Subway: 2, 3 to Grand Army Plaza or Q, S, B to Prospect Park or F to 15th St.–Prospect Park

SAVVY **TRAVELER**

Brooklyn Flea, a weekend market in both Fort Greene and on the waterfront at Williamsburg, captures Brooklyn's DIY spirit better than anything else. Hipsters, young families, and curious Manhattanites jostle among vendors selling jewelry, art, crafts, and more. One of the biggest draws, however, is the food: locally made pickles and granola, Salvadoran *pupusas* (stuffed corn-masa cakes), artisanal popsicles, and everything in between.

176 Lafayette Ave., between Clermont and Vanderbilt Aves.; 27 North 6th., between Kent Ave. and the East River www.brooklynflea.com, 718/935-1052

Park Slope

8 One of Brooklyn's most sought-after neighborhoods, Park Slope is well known for its stunning brownstones, popular music venues, and family-friendly eateries and stores. Head

Park Slope's Thistle Hill Tavern serves biodynamic wines and artisanal liquors.

northwest along Union Street and take a left on **Seventh Avenue,** one of the area's café-lined thoroughfares. Try **Thistle Hill Tavern** (*441 Seventh Ave.*) for an evening drink, and make sure to explore some of the quiet, scenic side streets. Those on the right lead toward **Fifth Avenue,** which in recent years has exploded with new boutiques and restaurants. Most are reliably good: **Juventino** (*370 Fifth Ave., 718/360-8469, $$$*), serving Mexican-inflected fare; **Campo de Fiori** (*187 Fifth Ave., 347/763-0933, $$*), a Roman-style trattoria; and **Brooklyn Fish Camp** (*162 Fifth Ave., 718/783-3264, $$$*), offering ultra-fresh seafood and warm service, are among the standouts. For late-night entertainment, check out nearby **Barbès** (*376 9th St., 347/422-0248*), which features eclectic musical acts, and **Southpaw** (*125 Fifth Ave., 718/230-0236*), a larger venue that hosts a range of emerging and world-famous artists.

Between Union St. and Prospect Expressway, and 4th Ave. and Prospect Park
• www.parkslope.com • Subway: D, N, R to Union St. or 4th Ave.–9th St.

Brooklyn Museum

One of the country's largest art museums has a world-class collection that ranges from Egyptian mummies to contemporary art.

For his show "Unbranded," Hank Willis Thomas made 41 photographs from media imagery.

Housed in a 560,000-square-foot (52,000 sq m) beaux arts building that recently gained a glass entrance pavilion, this venerable institution is sited right by Brooklyn Botanic Garden and has been at the heart of Brooklyn's cultural life since 1823. In addition to five floors of permanent installations embracing the world's cultures, special exhibitions showcase items from the collection that are rarely seen, as well as the work of such prominent artists as Annie Leibovitz and Haruki Murakami.

■ AFRICAN GALLERIES

Galleries on the first floor focus on West and Central African sculpture, including a **16th-century ivory gong** made for the king of Benin and a gorgeous 36-inch-tall (92 cm) **beaded Nigerian crown** of the late 1800s.

■ ISLAMIC GALLERIES

The encyclopedic Islamic displays on the second floor span a wide geographic area and range of objects. Among the most famous are several **Persian works** from the late 18th century, costumes from Turkmenistan, and the **"Battle of Karbala,"** a large Qajar-dynasty oil painting depicting the martyrdom of Husayn ibn Ali, the grandson of the prophet Muhammad.

■ EGYPTIAN GALLERIES

On the third floor, seven galleries chart the evolution of Egyptian art over four millennia. Highlights include a large chlorite **head of a princess; mummies** encased in intricately painted *cartonnages* (casings); and a **Book of the Dead** scroll. One of the oldest works in the museum is a **stylized female figure** from the Predynastic Period (3500–3400 B.C.).

■ ELIZABETH A. SACKLER CENTER FOR FEMINIST ART

The center of this unique fourth-floor exhibition of feminist art is **"The Dinner Party,"** an installation by Judy Chicago. This massive, triangular banquet has 39 place settings for important women from history, from the poet Sappho to the abolitionist and women's-rights activist Sojourner Truth.

■ LUCE CENTER FOR AMERICAN ART

This extensive exhibition on the fifth floor includes **American Identities: A New Look,** a fresh survey of American paintings, silver, and textiles from the colonial period to today. **Visible Storage** displays rare works usually held in storage, such as Tiffany lamps.

BROOKLYN

---

200 Eastern Parkway • www.brooklynmuseum.org • 718/638-5000 • $$ • Closed Mon., Tues., Jan. 1, Thanksgiving, and Dec. 25 • Subway: 2, 3 to Eastern Parkway–Brooklyn Museum

Bridges

As much an enduring symbol of New York as the city's other great structures, the Brooklyn Bridge was the first-ever bridge to link Manhattan Island to a populous outer borough (which, in the case of Brooklyn, was its own city at the time). Since then other mighty bridges have swung into place, overcoming the need to navigate the choppy waters, winter fogs, and freeze-ups on the city's waterways, and forging their own stories along the way.

A shared pedestrian and bike path runs along the center of the Brooklyn Bridge (above). The Ed Koch Queensboro Bridge, renamed after the former mayor in 2011 (right), is still known as Queensboro Bridge.

Spanning History

New York's 2,027 bridges (including 25 movable bridges) form a vital link in the city's infrastructure, carrying everything from cars, trucks, and subway trains to bicycles, pedestrians, and even water mains. The first to be built was the timber-decked King's Bridge in 1693, between Manhattan and the Bronx. It was demolished in 1917.

Oldest Structures

Highbridge (1843), the city's oldest bridge still standing, carries a water main across the Harlem River. The **Brooklyn Bridge** (see p. 162) is the oldest vehicle bridge. Opened in 1883, it was the world's longest span for more than 20 years—and like so many fabled structures, it's supposed to be cursed. Designer John Augustus Roebling died from injuries sustained while taking measurements for the towers. His son Washington was crippled by the bends while overseeing underwater work, but, determined to continue, he supervised the project from afar by watching through a telescope.

Breaking Records

The **Verrazano-Narrows,** with a central span of 4,260 feet (1,230 m), links Brooklyn and Staten Island and was named for Giovanni da Verrazano, who discovered what is now New York harbor in 1524. It was the world's longest suspension bridge when it opened in 1964. On the first Sunday of November, more than 40,000 runners shuffle across it at the start of the New York City Marathon. Verrazano-Narrows designer Othmar H. Ammann also engineered the **George Washington Bridge** (1931), which crosses the Hudson River between Manhattan's Upper West Side and New Jersey.

The **Ed Koch Queensboro Bridge** is the busiest, carrying some 180,000 vehicles daily between Manhattan and Queens across the East River. Completed in 1909, the bridge quickly earned New Yorkers' affections—novelist F. Scott Fitzgerald remarked how its perspective made Manhattan appear wildly beautiful.

Parks & Gardens

Central Park (see pp. 120–131) may be New York's premier green space, but it is far from the only place where you can get back to nature. The Manhattan landmark is only the fifth largest of the city's 29,000 public parks and gardens; the biggest, at 2,800 acres (1,133 ha), is the Staten Island Greenbelt.

■ BROOKLYN BOTANIC GARDEN
More than 10,000 plants from around the world fill the Brooklyn Botanic Garden (see pp. 164–165). Admire English cottage-garden planting in the **Shakespeare Garden,** or luxuriate in the warmth of the lush **Tropical Pavilion.**

■ PROSPECT PARK
Across Flatbush Avenue from the Brooklyn Botanic Garden lies Prospect Park (see p. 166), where Brooklyn's last stand of indigenous forest awaits. Summer concerts, a performing arts festival in June, and a winter ice-skating rink feature among the annual events.

■ GATEWAY NATIONAL
RECREATION AREA
Besides Prospect Park, Brooklyn's other large green space is Gateway National Recreation Area, which covers many of **Jamaica Bay's islands.**

Its 32 square miles (83 sq km) form a wildlife refuge. Opportunities for birding, walking, swimming, kayaking, picnicking, and fishing are legion.

www.nps.gov/gate • Jamaica Bay Wildlife Refuge: 718/318-4340 • Bus: Q21 from 116th St. (Rockaway)

■ THE NEW YORK
BOTANICAL GARDEN
Despite its inner-city reputation, the Bronx is surprisingly rich in parks. The New York Botanical Garden sprawls across 250 acres (100 ha) in the heart of the borough and is home to 50 distinct gardens and plant collections. They include the habitats housed in the **Enid A. Haupt Conservatory** and a stand of old growth New York forest (oak, birch, beech, and ash) that has never been logged.

Kazimiroff Blvd., Bronx River Parkway • www. nybg.org • 718/817-8700 • $$$$ • Closed Mon., and Dec 25 • Railroad: Metro–North Harlem line from Grand Central to Botanical Garden

BROOKLYN

The New York Botanical Garden's Victorian conservatory is the largest in the United States.

■ PELHAM BAY PARK

Wildlife is also a theme of this park on the Bronx's eastern edge. Pelham Bay includes inland areas and 13 miles (21 km) of shoreline on Long Island Sound. The park encompasses extensive woodland, saltwater marsh, and three islands. Explore the mainland sections by foot, bike, or horse along numerous trails, or navigate the coast by canoe. Visit **Thomas Pell Wildlife Sanctuary** for a chance to spot raccoons, coyotes, egrets, hawks, and many other species.

www.nycgovparks.org/parks • 718/430-1890 • Subway: IRT 6 to Pelham Bay Park

■ STATEN ISLAND GREENBELT

The city's most remote slice of parkland meanders through the middle and eastern parts of the island borough. The Staten Island Greenbelt comprises several contiguous green spaces including **High Rock** and **Willowbrook** parks, and 260-foot-high (79 m) **Moses' Mountain.** In addition to hiking and biking on six major trails (four of them woodland), visitors can partake in classes and events at the **Greenbelt Nature Center** (*700 Rockland Ave., 718/351-3450*).

www.sigreenbelt.org • 718/667-2165 • Ferry from Whitehall Terminal, Manhattan

PART 3

Travel Essentials

PLANNING YOUR TRIP

When To Go

The best months to see New York are September and October, when summer heat has eased and parks are full of fall color. Late spring is also a good choice—expect showers March to May, but with temperatures between 48°F and 68°F (9°C to 20°C). June through September averages 58°F to 83°F (14°C to 28°C), with July and August the hottest, most humid months. At this time, however, there are many outdoor attractions, such as concerts. The city looks beautiful in winter, and there are seasonal attractions such as ice skating and Christmas markets. Temperatures plummet from December to February, averaging from 23°F to 40°F (-5°C to 4°C). Whatever the season, you will be spending time both walking outdoors and exploring indoor attractions, so dress in layers year-round.

Visitor Information

New York City's **Visitor Information Center** (*www .nycgo.com, 212/484-1200*) has useful information. For a personalized introduction, contact **Big Apple Greeter** (*www.bigapplegreeter.org, 212/669-8159*). This nonprofit organization will match knowledgeable New Yorkers with visitors. Reserve two–three weeks in advance.

Useful Websites

www.nymag.com *New York* magazine, for listings of restaurants and entertainment.
www.mta.info Metropolitan Transit Authority, for schedules and maps of city subways and buses.
www.nyrestroom.com Lists public restrooms.

Notable Events & Festivals

JANUARY

Winter Antiques Show Seventh Regiment Armory, www.winterantiquesshow.com, 718/292-7392
Restaurant Week (all around town) www.nycgo.com

FEBRUARY

Chinatown Lunar New Year Parade www.betterchinatown.com
Westminster Kennel Club Dog Show Madison Square Garden, www.westminster kennelclub.org
Fashion Week http://nycfashioninfo.com

MARCH

St. Patrick's Day Parade Fifth Avenue, www.nyc stpatricksparade.org
Macy's Flower Show Herald Square, www.macys.com/ flowershow, 212/695-4400
Pier Antiques Show, Piers 92 and 94 in Midtown, www .stellashows.com, 973/808-5015

APRIL

Tribeca Film Festival www.tribecafilm.com, 219/941-2400

Baseball season New York Yankees, Yankee Stadium, www.yankees.mlbcom, 718/293-6000; New York Mets, Citi Field, www.mets.mlb.com, 718/507-8499
New York International Auto Show Jacob Javits Center, www.autoshowny.com, 800/282-3336

MAY

Bike New York, Five Borough Bike Tour www.bikenewyork .org, 212/932-2453 x 111
Fleet Week West Side Piers, www.fleetweeknewyork.com
Ninth Avenue Food Festival from 37th to 57th Streets, www.ninthavenuefoodfestival .com, 212/581-7029
Washington Square Outdoor Art Exhibit www.wsoae.org, 212/982-6255

JUNE

Museum Mile Festival Fifth Avenue from 82nd to 104th Streets, www.museum milefestival.org, 212/606-2296
Gay Pride March Fifth Avenue between 52nd Street and Greenwich Village, www. nycpride.org, 212/807-7433
Coney Island Mermaid Parade www.coneyisland.com, 718/372-5159

JULY

4th of July Dramatic fireworks display on the Hudson River 212/494-4495
Lincoln Center Festival www.lincolncenter.org, 212/721-6500
Restaurant Week (all around town) www.nycgo.com

AUGUST

Lincoln Center Out of Doors www.lincolncenter.org, 212/875-5766

U.S. Open Tennis Flushing Meadows Park, Queens, www.usopen.org, 866/6736-849

SEPTEMBER

West Indian-American Day Parade Eastern Parkway, Brooklyn, www.wiadca.com, 718/467-1797

New York Film Festival Lincoln Center, www.filmlinc.com, 212/875-5050

BAM Next Wave Festival Brooklyn Academy of Music, www.bam.org, 718/636-4100

Fashion Week http://nycfashioninfo.com

OCTOBER

Blessing of the Animals The Cathedral Church of St. John the Divine, www.stjohndivine.org, 212/316-7490

Greenwich Village Halloween Parade Sixth Ave., Spring St.–21st St., www.halloween-nyc.com

NOVEMBER

New York City Marathon www.ingnycmarathon.org, 212/423-2249

Radio City Christmas Spectacular www.radiocity.com, 212/307-1000

Macy's Thanksgiving Day Parade West 77th St. and Central Park West to 34th St. and Broadway, www.macys.com/parade, 212/494-4495

DECEMBER

Tree Lighting Rockefeller Center, www.rockefellercenter.com, 212/332-6868

Midtown Holiday Windows Fifth Avenue, between 42nd and 57th Streets, and Madison Avenue, between 55th and 60th Streets

New Year's Eve Times Square, www.timessquarenyc.org, 212/768-1560

GETTING FROM THE AIRPORTS

John F. Kennedy International Airport or **JFK** (www.jfkiat.com) is in southern Queens. **LaGuardia** (www.ifly.com/la-guardia-airport) on Long Island in Queens primarily serves North America. **Newark Liberty International Airport** (www.panynj.gov/airports/newark-liberty.html) is in Newark, New Jersey. **Air-Ride** provides recorded information on transportation to and from these airports (800/247-7433).

Buses

New York Airport Service has regular buses between JFK, LaGuardia, and Newark airports and Grand Central Terminal, Penn Station, and the Port Authority Bus Terminal (www.nyairportservice.com, 718/875-8200 x110). **SuperShuttle** runs between JFK and LaGuardia and most hotels (www.supershuttle.com, 800/258-3826). **Olympia Trails** runs between Newark airport and Midtown Manhattan (www.coachusa.com/olympia, 212/964-6233).

Car Services

Car companies offering pickups to and from the airport include **Carmel** (www.carmellimo.com, 212/666-6666 or 866/666-6666); and **Airlink,** hotel pickup for up to 11 passengers (www.goairlink shuttle.com, 877/599-8200). **Taxis** to and from JFK: flat rate of $45 to and from Manhattan, excluding tolls and tip; taxis to and from LaGuardia: by the meter, around $16–26, excluding tolls and tip; taxis from Newark: flat rate from $46, depending on destination, excluding tolls and tip. Book 24 hours in advance.

GETTING AROUND TOWN

As with many other great cities, there's no better way to experience New York than by using your own two feet. A car in Manhattan is more of a hindrance than a help, as traffic is always heavy and on-street parking hard to find. If you do drive into town, park your car at your hotel or a public garage ($20–$50 or more per day) and use the city's taxis, subways, and buses—they're the most convenient ways to get around the city.

Orienting Yourself

For the most part, the city's basic street grid makes it easy to navigate. In Manhattan numbered streets run east-west from First Street down in the East Village to 220th Street at the northern tip. Avenues run north-south and are numbered from First to Twelfth, increasing as you move west. However, Lexington, Madison, and Park Avenues fall between Third and Fifth Avenues, superseding Fourth Avenue. And, although maps and street signs refer to "The Avenue of the Americas," most New Yorkers still call it by its former name, Sixth Avenue.

Broadway meanders along the route of an old Indian trail and has little relation to the grid. And in much of Lower Manhattan, you'd do well to bring a compass: Streets angle off every which way, as they were laid out before the city planners took over.

Manhattan is divided into the East and West Sides, with Fifth Avenue the central axis.

If you're looking for a specific address, remember that building numbers advance out from Fifth Avenue on either side. So make sure you're clear what you're looking for: 300 *East* 23rd Street, for example, is very different from 300 *West* 23rd Street. Pay attention to the numbers of cross streets that often form part of an address to make it easier to find, such as 945 Madison Avenue at 75th Street.

Buses & Subways

Covering most of the city, buses and subway cars, at press time, cost $2.25 a ride with a MetroCard (see below)—half price for seniors and disabled, free for children under 3 feet 8 inches (1.1 m), including a transfer. Subways are ideal for long distances and

during rush hour. Buses can be scenic and relaxing but slow.
Lost and Found Buses and subways, *212/712-4500*.
MetroCards Available at all subway stations and at many newsstands. Fare is deducted each time you enter the subway or ride a bus; the card allows for a free transfer from the subway to or from a connecting bus within a two-hour period. Subways require MetroCards; buses take MetroCards or exact change.

Key Subway Routes

1: The 1 train takes you to sites on Broadway between 42nd Street and Manhattan's northern tip (including Times Square, Lincoln Center, Columbus Circle–Central Park, and the Cathedral Church of St. John the Divine).

R & W: These two trains are good for sites on Broadway from 42nd Street south to City Hall (including Times Square, Union Square, the Villages, and SoHo). They continue on to Wall Street and the island's historic southern tip.

C: The C is good for sites on the West Side between West 4th and 168th Streets (such as the High Line, Columbus Circle–Central Park, and the American Museum of Natural History). The legendary A express train travels the same route, but skips some stops that the C always makes.

6: This is your best option for sites on the East Side, from City Hall to 125th Street (including the East Village, Grand Central, the Met, and

the Guggenheim). The 4 and 5 also run express along this line.
L: The L runs east-west along 14th Street between First and Eighth Avenues.
S: This train runs east-west on 42nd Street from Grand Central Terminal to Times Square.

Mass Transit

Information: *www.mta.info, 718/330 1234.*

Public Transportation Tips

■ Some trains and buses are local, some express. Know where you're getting off to avoid overshooting your mark or waiting through many local stops unnecessarily.
■ Between Houston and 42nd Streets, any subway you catch (except the L and S; see Key Subway Routes) will be going north-south. To get across town in that area, a bus is your only public transportation option.
■ Buses only stop when someone wants to get on or off: Push the yellow strip along the wall to alert the bus driver your stop is coming up.
■ You'll find free subway maps at all stations and bus maps on the buses. Complete information is available at www.mta.info.

Taxis

Take only yellow cabs with the medallion numbers on the roof and the rates on the door. They are available if the medallion number is lit. The base fare is $2.50, then 40 cents for every additional fifth of a mile (four blocks) or every minute in

stopped or slow traffic. There's also a $1 peak-hour surcharge and a 50-cent night surcharge. There is no charge for other passengers or luggage. Tips are expected to be 15 percent.
NY Water Taxi *(www.nywater taxi.com)* runs ferries around Manhattan's perimeter and to the outer boroughs.

Hailing Taxis

To flag down one of New York's 11,787 licensed yellow cabs, station yourself along any busy avenue or street and start scanning for a rooftop light with its number illuminated. If it's out, the cab's taken. If the "off duty" lights are lit, the cabbie is going home. A raised arm is usually enough to get a cab, though you may be competing with other people. If somebody's got an arm up for an oncoming cab, don't try to steal it; the unwritten rule is first come, first served. Once inside, you'll find that your cabbie's expertise regarding side streets and traffic patterns is probably a lot better than his English. By the way, the annoying backseat TVs do have an "off" switch.

PRACTICAL ADVICE

The New York of today is a far cry from the New York of the 1970s, when crime was rampant and whole sections of the city were no-go zones. Now New York consistently ranks among the country's

safest large cities. That said, do keep a few things in mind:
- Don't give your bags to anyone in an airport or train/bus station other than authorized personnel.
- Only take official yellow taxis from the airport. Their rates are set by the city, unlike those of the "gypsy cab" operators.
- Carry your wallet in a place you can be constantly mindful of (not a back pocket), and be sure all bags are always securely closed and in your possession, even in restaurants and stores.
- Many of the panhandlers you'll see on the streets and subways are well-practiced professionals. Don't feel guilty or intimidated into giving; you can say, "Sorry, no."
- Have a clear idea of where you're going when visiting the outer boroughs. The streets aren't laid out as logically as in Manhattan, most are named rather than numbered, it can be challenging to hail a taxi, and subways aren't as easy to find. At night, some areas can get uncomfortably desolate.
- While city parks aren't necessarily dangerous at night, you'll want to tune your awareness up an extra notch. Use common sense when it comes to particularly dark or empty sections.
- When using the subways at night, make a point of riding the center cars, which are usually more crowded.
- Be aware of those around you when using ATMs, and don't count your money on the street.

TRAVELERS WITH DISABILITIES

Airport Travelers' Aid *718/656-4870.*
Asser Levy Playground has a playground for disabled children and a free outdoor pool *(East 23rd St. at Asser Levy Place, near the East River, www .nycgovparks.org/parks/asserlevy, 212/447-2020).*
Big Apple Greeter *(www .bigapplegreeter.org, 212/669-8159)* offers information for disabled travelers and tours led by volunteers.
HAI (Hospital Audiences, Inc.) gives a guide to access in New York's cultural institutions and provides theater services for the blind *(www.hospitalaudiences.org, 212/575-7676).*
Lighthouse International has Braille maps and events devised by and for the visually impaired *(111 East 59th St. www .lighthouse.org, 800/829-0500, 212/821-9713).*

EMERGENCIES

In an emergency, call *911.*
- Crime Victims Hotline, *212/577-7777.*
- Poison Control Center, *800/222-1222.*
- Medical emergencies: Proceed to the nearest emergency room (call *411* for the nearest hospital) or call *911* for an ambulance.

HOTELS

The selection and price range of places to stay in New York is remarkably varied, with options to meet every taste and budget. There are as many bargains available as in any other place, with low-cost options that include bed-and-breakfasts and small older hotels in some of the most interesting neighborhoods. Check out which part of the city you'll be spending most of your vacation in, and find a hotel to match your budget. You may wish to spend a few days in an inexpensive place and then splurge on one night in one of the city's most luxurious hotels. Also try to reserve in advance, as some of the best rooms can fill up early.

TRAVEL ESSENTIALS

Once you determine your total room budget, decide what neighborhood or area appeals to you and then research in depth. From Lower Manhattan to the Upper East and West Sides and beyond, the city teems with shopping, sight-seeing, and cultural and historic attractions. If you are drawn more to Broadway or other West Side attractions, then a place in the Times Square or Lincoln Center area may be best.

Be sure to calculate transportation into both your time and money budgets. Taxis are usually available, but a ride from the West Village to the Upper East Side, for example, can be quite expensive and also—depending on traffic—slow. If you have limited time in the city, choosing a hotel by location is imperative, to avoid spending half your trip in subways or stuck in traffic.

For disabled access, it is recommended you check with the hotel to establish the extent of its facilities. Also verify parking or access to parking spaces. Most New York hotels are air-conditioned.

Organization

Hotels listed here have been grouped first according to neighborhood, then listed alphabetically by price range.

Credit Card Abbreviations:

AE (American Express); DC (Diner's Club); MC (Mastercard); V (Visa).

Price Range

HOTELS

An indication of the cost of a double room in the high season is given by **$** signs.

$$$$$ Over $325
$$$$ $260–$325
$$$ $200–$260
$$ $140–$200
$ Under $140

Text Symbols

- ℹ️ No. of Guest Rooms
- 🚇 Subway
- 🏊 Outdoor Pool
- 💪 Health Club
- 💳 Credit Cards Accepted

LOWER MANHATTAN

■ Hotel on Rivington
$$$$$
107 RIVINGTON STREET
(BETWEEN LUDLOW
AND ESSEX STREETS)
TEL 212/475-2600
www.hotelonrivington.com
This 21-story glass tower in the historic Lower East Side offers terrific city views from the floor-to-ceiling glass windows in every room. Cutting-edge designers injected creativity into all aspects of the hotel's concept and chic look. Many of the rooms have balconies, and unusual amenities include Japanese soaking tubs and in-room spa services. For food, drink, and socializing, try Thor, the first-floor restaurant, bar, and lounge.
ℹ️ 94 rooms, 16 suites 🚇 F to Delancey, J to Essex St.
💳 All major cards

■ Millennium Hilton
$$$$$
55 CHURCH STREET
TEL 212/693-2001
www.hilton.com
This top-end Financial District destination, alongside the World Trade Center site, gleams

with high-tech style. There is a plasma TV and high-speed internet access in each room, a gym, pool, cocktail bar, Church & Dey restaurant, and some beautiful views of New York Harbor. Lower rates are available on weekends.

🛈 561 🚇 1 to Cortlandt St.; C to World Trade Center 🔁 📺 💳 All major cards

■ SoHo Grand
$$$$$
310 W. BROADWAY (BETWEEN GRAND & CANAL STREETS)
TEL 212/965-3000 OR 800/965-3000
www.sohogrand.com
A striking design and a fashionable, pet-friendly destination greets those who enjoy the downtown vantage point. Endless interesting stores and galleries are within walking distance.

🛈 367 + 4 suites 🚇 A, C, E to Canal St. 📺 💳 All major cards

■ Gild Hall
$$$
15 GOLD STREET (AT PLATT STREET)
TEL 212/232-7700
www.thompsonhotels.com
Jammed full of contemporary design, the Gild Hall is a departure from the more traditional hotels clustered around the Financial District. Among its attractions are a library bar spread over two levels, an elegant champagne bar, and mini-bars furnished by one of New York's top gourmet markets Dean & Deluca.

🛈 126 🚇 2, 3 to Fulton St. 💳 All major cards

THE VILLAGES

■ The Cooper Square Hotel
$$$$$
25 COOPER SQUARE (BOWERY AND FIFTH STREET)
TEL 212/475-5700
www.thecoopersquarehotel .com
A chic new hotel whose curved, glassy, 21-story tower was built around an 1845 tenement building. Super-stylish rooms blend a minimalist aesthetic with natural woods, plus views from floor-to-ceiling windows.

🚇 145 🚇 A, C, E, to Canal St. 💳 All major cards

■ Gramercy Park Hotel
$$$$$
2 LEXINGTON AVENUE (AT EAST 21ST STREET)
TEL 212/920-5890
www.gramercyparkhotel.com
Modern bohemia defines the Gramercy Park Hotel, adorned with modern art masterpieces and antique furniture. Rooms are decorated in a vivid Renaissance color palette inspired by Raphael. The real draw, though, is the access it offers guests to Gramercy Park, Manhattan's most coveted private green space.

🚇 185 🚇 4, 6 to 23rd St. 💳 All major cards

■ Hotel Gansevoort
$$$$$
18 NINTH AVE. (BETWEEN LITTLE WEST 12TH AND 13TH STREETS)
TEL 212/206-6700
www.hotelgansevoort.com
This 187-room hotel in the Meatpacking District offers spectacular views of the city and the Hudson River from its

room balconies and 45-foot (13.7 m) heated rooftop pool. Guests can be pampered at the huge spa, sip cocktails in the Plunge Rooftop Bar & Lounge, savor Japanese cuisine in the Tanuki Tavern, and spin around the city on the hotel's complimentary bicycles.

🛈 187 🚇 A, C, E, L to 14th St. 💳 All major cards

■ Tribeca Grand Hotel
$$$$$
2 SIXTH AVENUE
TEL 212-519-6600
www.tribecagrand.com
With a grand atrium inspired by European cathedrals and mid-20th-century public buildings, the Tribeca Grand features a private screening room that makes it a favorite of celebrities. The rooms combine modernist design with warm earth tones. Be sure to have a drink or two in the bar to maximize your celebrity-spotting chances.

🛈 203 🚇 6 to Astor Pl. 💳 All major cards

■ Abingdon Guest House
$$$
13 EIGHTH AVENUE (BETWEEN 12TH AND JANE STREETS)
TEL 212/243-5384
www.abingdonguesthouse.com
A charming, gracious B&B occupies two Federal-style 1850s town houses in relaxed Greenwich Village. The rooms, each with private bath, are individually decorated in bold colors and furnished in elegant, yet cozy style.

🛈 9 🚇 A, C, E to 14th St. 💳 All major cards

■ Washington Square Hotel
$$
**103 WAVERLY PLACE
(AT MACDOUGAL STREET)
TEL 212/777-9515 OR
800/222-0418**
www.wshotel.com
Steps away from Washington Square Park in Greenwich Village, this renovated, century-old hotel has art-deco-inspired rooms, an excellent restaurant, and a lobby bar where guests can take tea or try cocktails while making use of the Wi-Fi access.

🛈 180 🚇 A, B, C, D, E, F to W. 4th St. 🍴 🏧 All major cards

■ Larchmont Hotel
$
**27 WEST 11TH STREET (BETWEEN FIFTH AND SIXTH AVENUES)
TEL 212/989-9333
FAX 212/989-9496**
www.larchmonthotel.com
Tiny but pleasant rooms in this European-style hotel come with continental breakfast included, and a home-away-from-home feel. Bathrooms are shared.

🛈 50 🚇 F to 14th St. 🏧 AE, MC, V

MIDTOWN SOUTH

■ The Inn at Irving Place
$$$$$
**56 IRVING PLACE (BETWEEN 17TH AND 18TH STREETS)
TEL 212/533-4600 OR
800/685-1447**
www.innatirving.com
Two unmarked 1834 town houses make up this gracious, Victorian-style hotel in the heart of Gramercy Park. Rooms are furnished with antiques and four-poster beds, and have Wi-Fi access. Dine at the

Spanish wine bar and restaurant or try the four-course tea at Lady Mendl's Tea Salon.

🛈 11 suites 🚇 4, 5, 6 to Union Sq. 🏧 All major cards

■ Morgans New York
$$$$$
**237 MADISON AVENUE
TEL 212/686-0300**
www.morganshotel.com
There's no sign out front and design is minimalist in this hotel, its colors subdued grays, black, and white. But this peaceful retreat, opened in 1984 by Studio 54 creators Ian Schrager and Steve Rubell, now packs a punch: Asia de Cuba, the first-floor restaurant, is pristine white but flashy, its focus a long share-table in the center, with a waterfall hologram above. Celebrities and famous athletes flock here.

🛈 113 🚇 4, 5, 6 to Grand Central 🍴 Nearby 🏧 All major cards

■ The Standard
$$$$
**848 WASHINGTON STREET
(AT 13TH STREET)
TEL 212/645-4646**
www.standardhotels.com
It's all about the views at this André Balazs hotel, which straddles the new High Line park in the hip Meatpacking District, just one block from the Hudson River. The building's exterior is reminiscent of international-style landmarks like the UN building, while its streamlined rooms are 21st-century modern. All are angled to maximize the views.

🛈 337 🚇 A, C, E to 14th St. 🏧 All major cards

■ St. Giles Hotel–
The Tuscany
$$$$
**120 EAST 39TH STREET
TEL 212/686-1600**
www.stgileshotels.com
A stylish boutique hotel with a superb location has wonderful amenities and extra-spacious rooms with marble bathrooms.

🛈 110 + 12 suites 🚇 4, 5, 6 to Grand Central 🍴 🏧 All major cards

■ The Gershwin Hotel
$$$–$$$$
**7 EAST 27TH STREET
(BETWEEN FIFTH AND MADISON AVENUES)
TEL 212/545-8000**
www.gershwinhotel.com
This 100-year-old spot in the city's old "Tin Pan Alley" area (home to hit 1930s and '40s songwriters) caters to budget-conscious and creative global travelers. Rooms range from shared-bathroom dorms to private rooms and suites. Pop culture is the muse here.

🛈 140 + 10 dorm rooms 🚇 6, N, R, W to 28th St. 🏧 AE, MC, V

■ Hotel Chelsea
$$$
**222 WEST 23RD STREET
(BETWEEN SEVENTH AND EIGHTH AVENUES)
TEL 212/243-3700**
www.hotelchelsea.com
The historic home of artists and writers has a cozy lobby filled with art. It's definitely worth a look even if no rooms are available.

🛈 400 🚇 1 to 23rd St.; C, E to 23rd St. 🍴 Nearby 🏧 All major cards

■ Hotel Metro
$$$
**45 WEST 35TH STREET
(BETWEEN FIFTH AND SIXTH
AVENUES)
TEL 212/947-2500 OR
800/356-3870**
www.hotelmetronyc.com
Deluxe guest rooms join forces
with a roof terrace that has
views of the nearby Empire
State Building. Also available
are a fitness center, library, and
restaurant. The main Midtown
sights are just minutes away.
🛈 *155 + 20 suites* 🚇 *1, 2, 3 to 34th
St.* 🅿️ 💳 *All major cards*

MIDTOWN NORTH

■ The Algonquin
$$$$$
**59 WEST 44TH STREET (BETWEEN
FIFTH AND SIXTH AVENUES)
TEL 212/840-6800 OR
888-304-2047**
www.algonquinhotel.com
This official literary landmark
has been entertaining writers
since the 1920s. Enjoy the
glamour of the paneled Supper
Club room and cocktails in the
lobby. Rooms are charming, the
locale is ideal, and guests' needs
are noted for the next visit.
🛈 *175* 🚇 *B, D, F to 42nd St.*
💳 *All major cards*

■ Four Seasons
$$$$$
**57 EAST 57TH STREET (BETWEEN
PARK AND MADISON AVENUES)
TEL 212/758-5700**
www.fourseasons.com
This 52-story, art deco–style
monument designed by I. M.
Pei and completed in 1993 has
received top ratings and boasts
the largest rooms in the city,
with accompanying big views.
Expect modernistic furniture,
giant Florentine marble
bathrooms, and elaborate
bedside push-button systems.
🛈 *370* 🚇 *4, 5, 6, N, R to 59th St.*
🅿️ 💳 *All major cards*

■ Jumeirah Essex House
$$$$$
**160 CENTRAL PARK SOUTH
(BETWEEN SIXTH AND SEVENTH
AVENUES)
TEL 212/247-0300 OR
888/645-5697**
www.jumeirahessexhouse.com
Now part of a Dubai-based
luxury chain, Essex House
completed a $90-million
refurbishment in late 2007
that conserved its dramatic art
deco setting and added high-
tech, environmentally friendly
features. The hotel has stunning
views of Central Park.
🛈 *516 + 81 suites* 🚇 *1, A, C, B, D
to Columbus Circle–59th St.; N, R,
Q, W to 57th St.* 🅿️
💳 *All major cards*

■ The Peninsula
$$$$$
**700 FIFTH AVENUE
(AT 55TH STREET)
TEL 212/956-2888 OR
800/262-9467**
www.peninsula.com
A turn-of-the-20th-century
beaux arts landmark offers
views down Fifth Avenue,
art nouveau furnishings, and
oversized beds and bathrooms.
More luxury awaits at the
rooftop spa and outdoor
rooftop Pen-Top Bar and
Terrace, excellent for summer-
time cocktails and city views.
🛈 *250* 🚇 *E, V to 5th Ave./53rd St.; F
to 57th St.* 🅿️ 🏊 💳 *All major cards*

■ The Plaza
$$$$$
**CENTRAL PARK SOUTH
768 FIFTH AVENUE
(AT 59TH STREET)
TEL 212/759-3000**
www.fairmont.com/theplaza
The hotel's 282 suites and
rooms include the suite
where the beloved children's
book character Eloise has
"lived" since 1955. The Grand
Ballroom, Palm Court (with
Tiffany ceiling), Oak Room, and
Oak Bar are among its historic
features, and guests should
make a point of strolling the
exterior grounds at the corner
of Central Park.
🛈 *282* 🚇 *N, R, W to 5th Ave./
59th St.* 🅿️ 💳 *All major cards*

■ The Ritz-Carlton
$$$$$
**50 CENTRAL PARK SOUTH
(AT SIXTH AVENUE)
TEL 212/308-9100 OR
800/241-3333**
www.ritzcarlton.com
Formerly the St. Moritz, this
33-story luxury hotel offers
glamour, a great location,
butlers, and fabulous lounges.
The atelier restaurant serves
innovative French cuisine.
🛈 *261* 🚇 *F to 57th St.*
💳 *All major cards*

■ St. Regis
$$$$$
**2 EAST 55TH STREET (BETWEEN
FIFTH AND MADISON AVENUES)
TEL 212/753-4500**
**www.starwoodhotels.com
/stregis**
This restored 1904 beaux arts
gem has elegant yet accessible
public rooms and the finest
service and amenities. Enjoy

the riches of Lespinasse, one of New York's top restaurants, and of the great King Cole Bar, dominated by the engaging Maxfield Parrish mural of the king himself.

ⓘ 322 🚍 E, V, to 5th Ave./53rd St.; N, R, W to 5th Ave./59th St. 🍴 🏧 All major cards

■ The Shoreham
$$$$$
33 WEST 55TH STREET (BETWEEN FIFTH AND SIXTH AVENUES)
TEL 212/247-6700 OR
800/553-3347
www.shorehamhotel.com

A lavish refurbishment of this boutique hotel has created individually styled rooms with slate and marble bathrooms, a Technogym fitness center, and a bar with an underwater feel.

ⓘ 47 + 37 suites 🚍 E, V to 5th Ave./53rd St.; N, Q, R W to 57th St./7th Ave. 🍴 Nearby 🏧 All major cards

■ The Waldorf-Astoria & Waldorf Towers
$$$$–$$$$$
301 PARK AVENUE
(AT 50TH STREET)
TEL 212/355-3000
www.waldorfastoriacollection.com

The great Waldorf-Astoria is one of the quintessential New York hotels. The art deco lobby is magnificent, and the elaborately appointed Waldorf Towers (floors 28–42) provide quarters for visiting presidents. The French restaurant, Peacock Alley, receives lavish praise.

ⓘ 1410 🚍 6 to 51st St. or E, V to Lexington Ave./53rd St. 🍴 🏧 All major cards

■ Casablanca Hotel
$$$$
147 WEST 43RD STREET
(BETWEEN SIXTH AVENUE AND BROADWAY)
TEL 212/869-1212 OR
888/922-7225
www.casablancahotel.com

They're serious about the name, with Moroccan touches mixing with modern, a guest lounge called Rick's Café, and a vaguely North African outdoor courtyard. This hotel is great for theatergoers.

ⓘ 40 + 8 suites 🚍 1, 2, 3, 7 to Times Sq.–42nd St. 🍴 🏧 All major cards

■ The Mansfield
$$$$
12 WEST 44TH STREET (BETWEEN FIFTH AND SIXTH AVENUES)
TEL 212/944-6050 OR
877/847-4444
www.mansfieldhotel.com

A former bachelor's residence includes a library with chess by the fireplace and complimentary coffee, pillowtop mattresses, a modern gym, a bar with regular live music, and a romantic late-19th-century ambience.

ⓘ 103 + 26 suites 🚍 B, D, F to 42nd St.; 1, 2, 3, 7 to Times Sq. 🍴 Nearby 🏧 All major cards

■ Millennium UN Hotel
$$$$
1 UNITED NATIONS PLAZA 44TH STREET (BETWEEN FIRST AND SECOND AVENUES)
TEL 212/758-1234 OR
866-866-8086
www.millenniumhotels.com

The award-winning twin-towered modern building rises high above the East Side. Staying here puts you in the midst of global drama, as diplomats and

staff rush to meetings or to their offices on the first 27 floors of the UN Plaza. Hotel rooms—all with stunning views—start on the 28th floor. Artworks from New York City and various nations are found throughout the hotel. The excellent sports facilities include indoor tennis courts and a pool. A shuttle services city sites and the airports.

ⓘ 428 G4, 5, 6, 7 to 42nd St. 🚇 🍴 🏧 All major cards

■ The New York Palace
$$$$
455 MADISON AVENUE
(AT 50TH STREET)
TEL 212/888-7000 OR
800/697-2522
www.newyorkpalace.com

Located in what was originally the 1882 Stanford White–designed Villard Houses, this landmark site has retained its opulence through various incarnations. Its elegantly furnished 55-story tower overlooks St. Patrick's Cathedral. Fine places for food and drink on-site include Istana Restaurant and Gilt, just inside the courtyard.

ⓘ 600 🚍 E, F to 5th Ave.; B, D, F to Rockefeller Center 🍴 🏧 All major cards

■ The Paramount
$$$$
235 WEST 46TH STREET
(BETWEEN BROADWAY AND EIGTH AVENUE)
TEL 212/764-5500 OR
888/741-5600
www.nycparamount.com

A Philippe Starck–designed lobby, playful, attractive decor, and location in the heart of the theater district are among this

TRAVEL ESSENTIALS

hotel's pluses. Try for one of the recently renovated rooms.

🛈 601 + 12 suites 🚇 1, 2, 3, 7 to 42nd St.–Times Sq. 🛗
🏧 All major cards

■ Roger Smith
$$$–$$$$
501 LEXINGTON AVENUE (BETWEEN 47TH AND 48TH STREETS)
TEL 212/755-1400
www.rogersmith.com
This casual 1929 boutique hotel has a strong arts orientation, with an in-house gallery and performance space. Continental breakfast is included.

🛈 130 🚇 E, V to Lexington Ave./53rd St.; 6 to 51st St.
🏧 All major cards

■ Hotel Elysée
$$$
60 EAST 54TH STREET (BETWEEN MADISON AND PARK AVENUES)
TEL 212/753-1066 OR 800/535-9733
www.elyseehotel.com
Thirties' decor, charming rooms, a small roof terrace, and evening wine and cheese make this boutique hotel both luxurious and personal.

🛈 88 + 11 suites 🚇 E, V to Lexington Ave.; 6 to 51st St.
🛗 🏧 All major cards

UPPER EAST SIDE

■ The Carlyle
$$$$$
35 EAST 76TH STREET
TEL 212/744-1600 OR 800-227-5737
www.thecarlyle.com
Since 1931 this gemlike hotel has welcomed the world's

elite in a grand European style. Rooms have antiques, marble bathrooms with whirlpools, and state-of-the-art electronics. Nancy Reagan and the late President Kennedy were regular guests. Those who do not check in may still partake of romantic dining in the Carlyle Restaurant, bistro entertainment in the Café Carlyle, or tea in the Gallery, modeled after Turkey's Topkapi Palace.

🛈 190 + 65 residential apartments
🚇 6 to 77th St. 🏧 All major cards

■ Hôtel Plaza Athénée
$$$$$
37 EAST 64TH STREET (BETWEEN PARK AND MADISON AVENUES)
TEL 212/734-9100
www.plaza-athenee.com
Louis XVI decor stars at this New York version of the Paris original, distinguished by its smaller size and location on a quiet residential block close by Central Park. Deluxe suites have atriums and balconies.

🛈 149 🚇 6 to 68th St. 🛗
🏧 All major cards

■ The Lowell
$$$$$
28 EAST 63RD STREET (BETWEEN PARK AND MADISON AVENUE)
TEL 212/838-1400 OR 800/221-4444
www.lowellhotel.com
A 1920s historic landmark on a quiet street, provides tasteful, Old World charm in an intimate setting. Many rooms have working fireplaces, kitchens, and libraries.

🛈 61 🚇 4, 5, 6 to 59th St. 🛗
🏧 All major cards

■ The Mark
$$$$$
25 EAST 77TH STREET (BETWEEN FIFTH AND MADISON AVENUES)
TEL 212/744-4300 OR 800/843-6275
www.themarkhotel.com
An elegant location with formal decor, large rooms with marble or ceramic baths, high-quality artwork, and luxurious amenities. The wood-paneled Mark Restaurant is perfect for indulgent afternoon teas.

🛈 180 🚇 6 to 77th St. 🛗
🏧 All major cards

■ The Pierre
$$$$$
2 EAST 61ST STREET (AT FIFTH AVENUE)
TEL 212/838-8000 OR 800/7437734
www.tajhotels.com
Elegance, antiques, and opulent decor characterize this hotel overlooking Central Park that dates from the 1930s. Its recent $100-million renovation added a Jiva spa. Rooms are high-ceilinged and decorated in cool, restful colors, with furnishings in rich silks and brocades.

🛈 206 🚇 N, R to 5th Ave. 🛗
🏧 All major cards

■ The Regency
$$$$$
540 PARK AVENUE (AT 61ST STREET)
TEL 212/759-4100
www.loewshotels.com
Named for its Regency decor, this hotel has both understated elegance and every amenity, including TVs and phones beside the marble bathtubs.

🛈 288 + 74 suites 🚇 4, 5, 6 to 59th St. 🛗 🏧 All major cards

HOTELS

■ The Sherry-Netherland
$$$$$
781 FIFTH AVENUE
(AT 59TH STREET)
TEL 212/355-2800 OR
877-743-7710
www.sherrynetherland.com
This exclusive 1927 apartment hotel at the edge of Central Park numbers among its many attractions a lobby modeled on the Vatican library and guest elevators that once graced the Vanderbilt Mansion. Suites include separate living and dining areas. The fitness center is state-of-the-art, and a recent renovation injected the legendary restaurant, Harry Cipriani, with a new look.
ⓘ 53 **🚇** N, R, W to 5th Ave/ 59th St. **💳** All major cards

■ Gracie Inn
$$$$
502 EAST 81ST STREET (BETWEEN YORK AND EAST END AVENUES)
TEL 212/628-1700
www.gracieinnhotel.com
This B&B in a former family residence offers 13 rustic-style rooms of various sizes, each with kitchenette, full bath, and cable—a real haven in a quiet location near Carl Schurz Park, in easy reach of Museum Mile.
ⓘ 12 **🚇** 4, 5, 6 to 86th St. **💳** All major cards

■ The Franklin Hotel
$$$
164 EAST 87TH STREET (BETWEEN LEXINGTON AND THIRD AVENUES)
TEL 212/369-1000 OR
800/607-4009
www.franklinhotel.com
Pet friendly and romantic, the Franklin offers nicely decorated rooms with canopy beds, custom furniture, and photos of the city. There are complimentary wine-and-cheese receptions nightly.
ⓘ 53 **🚇** 4, 5, 6 to 86th St. **💳** AE, MC, V

■ Hotel Wales
$$$
1295 MADISON AVENUE
(AT 92ND STREET)
TEL 212/876-6000 OR
877/847-4444
www.waleshotel.com
This early-20th-century-style haven has spacious suites a block from Central Park. Guests can dine at Paola's, the on-site Italian bistro, or order room service from Sarabeth's on the ground floor.
ⓘ 45 + 47 suites **🚇** 6 to 96th St. **💳** AE, MC, V

UPPER WEST SIDE

■ Trump International Hotel & Towers
$$$$$
1 CENTRAL PARK WEST (AT COLUMBUS CIRCLE, BETWEEN 60TH AND 61ST STREETS)
TEL 212/299-1000 OR
888/448-7867
www.trumpintl.com
Donald Trump's mega-venture at the tip of Central Park, featuring floor-to-ceiling windows and personal attachés assigned to guests to coordinate their lives in New York. Dine downstairs at Nougatine or Jean Georges, or have one of the chefs cook for you in your suite.
ⓘ 176 suites **🚇** 1, A, B, C, D to Columbus Circle–59th St. **🍽** **💳** All major cards

■ Country Inn the City
$$$
WEST 77TH STREET
(BETWEEN BROADWAY AND WEST END AVENUE)
TEL 212/580-4183
www.countryinnthecity.com
This nicely restored 19th-century town house has lovely, self-contained apartments with kitchens. Delis, parks, museums, and a market are all nearby. No elevator.
ⓘ 4 **🚇** 1 to 79th St.

■ The Excelsior Hotel
$$$
45 WEST 81ST STREET
(BETWEEN COLUMBUS AVENUE AND CENTRAL PARK WEST)
TEL 212/362-9200 OR
800/368-4575
www.excelsiorhotelny.com
Right next to the American Museum of Natural History, the hotel offers large, comfortable rooms, some with views of Central Park. Many Upper West Side sites are minutes away, and those of the Upper East Side just a stroll across the park.
ⓘ 200 **🚇** 1 to 79th St.; C, B to 81st St. **💳** AE, MC, V

■ Hotel Beacon NYC
$$$
2130 BROADWAY
(AT 75TH STREET)
TEL 212/787-1100
OR 800/572-4969
www.beaconhotel.com
Generously sized rooms, a great central location, and a family-friendly ethos characterize this hotel. All rooms and suites have marble bathrooms and fully equipped kitchenettes.
ⓘ 248 suites **🚇** 1, 2, 3 to 72nd St. **🍽** Nearby **💳** All major cards

■ The Lucerne
$$$
**201 WEST 79TH STREET
(AT AMSTERDAM AVENUE)
TEL 212/875-1000**
www.thelucernehotel.com
Classic rooms in a gorgeously
renovated 1904 landmark
building combine with a location
close to Central Park and a
popular restaurant and sidewalk
café frequented by locals. Guests
can enjoy the complimentary
wine hour on Thursday evenings.
🛈 184 🚇 1 to 79th St. 💳 AE, MC, V

■ The Hotel Newton
$$
**2528 BROADWAY
TEL 212/678-6500**
www.thehotelnewton.com
Comfortable guest rooms include
de luxe suites with kitchenettes.
The location is excellent for
prime sightseeing, and strolls
to Riverside and Central Parks.
Friendly staff will help with queries
and bookings. Dining options
abound, the nearest being the
Manhattan Diner next door.
🛈 117 🚇 1,2,3 to 96th St.

■ West End Studios
$
**850 WEST END AVENUE
(BETWEEN WEST 102ND STREET
AND WEST 101ST STREET)
TEL 212/749-7104
FAX 212/865-5130**
www.westendstudios.com
A smart yet affordable hotel is
located just a few blocks away
from Riverside Park, close to
many great eateries, and a
short taxi ride from Broadway's
theaters. The hotel offers clean,
basic rooms with cable TVs.
🛈 85 🚇 1 to 103rd St.
💳 All major cards

HARLEM

■ Harlem Renaissance House
$$
**237 WEST 109TH STREET
TEL 212/226-1590**
**www.harlemrenaissancehouse
.com**
A fully restored Stanford White
brownstone offers two large
rooms, each with a bathroom,
and use of the breakfast foyer
(with piano), dining room,
parlor with balcony, and library.
🛈 2 🚇 B, C, 2, 3 to 135th St.
💳 AE, MC, V; cash only on check-in

BROOKLYN

■ Brooklyn Marriot
$$$$$
**333 ADAMS STREET
TEL 718/246-7000**
www.marriott.com
A luxury hotel just across the
river from Lower Manhattan.
Situated close to the Brooklyn
Bridge near the historic Brooklyn
Heights neighborhood.
🛈 638 + 28 suites 🚇 A, C, F to
Jay St. 🍴 💳 All major cards

■ At Home in Brooklyn
$$
**15 PROSPECT PARK WEST
(BETWEEN CARROLL STREET AND
PRESIDENT STREET)
TEL 718/622-5292**
www.athomeinbrooklyn.com
Four rooms in this old mansion
facing Prospect Park provide a
European-style base. The owners
promote an authentic Brooklyn
experience and can offer real
insights into the surrounding area.
The entire house can be rented
for a stay of more than a week.
🛈 4 🚇 2, 3, 4 to Grand Army Plaza

■ The Sofia Inn
$$
**288 PARK PLACE
(AT VANDERBILT AVENUE)
TEL 917/865-7428**
**www.brooklynbedand
breakfast.net**
This charming bed and
breakfast in a 1901 Brooklyn
brownstone is owned by a
former cab driver. The Inn
has a small number of quirky,
individually decorated rooms.
🛈 4 + 2 suites 🚇 2, 3, 4 to
Grand Army Plaza 🍴 Nearby
💳 All major cards

AIRPORT HOTELS

■ Best Western City View Motor Inn
$$$
**33–17 GREENPOINT AVENUE,
LONG ISLAND CITY
TEL 718/392-8400
OR 800/780-7234**
www.bestwesternnewyork.com
A converted 19th-century public
school near the New York Mets'
new Citi Field stadium and U.S
Open Tennis Center. Free shuttle
to and from LaGuardia.
🛈 72 🚇 7 to 40th Street 🍴 Nearby
💳 All major cards

■ Sheraton LaGuardia East Hotel
$$$
**135-20 39TH AVENUE
TEL 212/299-1000 OR
888/448-7867**
**www.starwoodhotels.com/
sheraton**
Modern airport hotel near the
U.S. Open Tennis Center and
the Mets' new Citi Field.
🛈 173 suites 🚇 7 to Main St. Flushing
🍴 💳 All major cards

INDEX

Page numbers in *italic* refer to
  map pages

A

The Abyssinian Baptist Church
  149, 153
airport hotels 187
airports 177
Algonquin Hotel 17, 67, 183
American Family Immigration
  History Center 51
American Folk Art Museum *135*, 139
American Museum of Natural
  History *32*, 35, *134*, 140–141
Apollo Theater *149*, 152
architecture
  art deco 94, 98–99
  Brooklyn Heights 162–163
  brownstones 142–143
  Armory Show 117
art deco 94, 98–99
art museums *see* museums
Asia Society and Museum 53

B

bars & cocktails 27, 84–85
Battery Park *42*, 44
Belvedere Castle *123*, 126
Big Apple Greeter 176
biking 130, 173
Bloomingdale's 118
bridges 162, 170–171
Brooklyn *39*, 69, 158–171, *160–161*
  Brooklyn Botanic Garden *161*,
    164–165, 172
  Brooklyn Bridge *160*, 162, 170
  Brooklyn Heights' Historic Houses
    160, 162–163
  Brooklyn Heights Promenade *160*,
    163–164
  Brooklyn Museum *161*,
    168–169
  Central Library *161*, 165
  hotels 187
  Park Slope *160*, 166–167
  Prospect Park *161*, 166, 172
brownstones 142–143
Bryant Park 81, 101
buses 178

C

Carl Schurz Park *105*, 110–111

Castle Clinton National
  Monument 44
The Cathedral Church of St. John
  the Divine *149*, 151
Central Library *161*, 165
Central Park *14*, 17, *18*, *38–39*,
    120–127, *122–123*
  Belvedere Castle *122*, 126
  Central Park Zoo *33*, 35, *123*, 124
  Conservatory Garden *122*, 127
  Loeb Boathouse *123*, 125
  The Mall *123*, 124
  Shakespeare Garden *122*, 127
  Strawberry Fields *123*, 126
children, New York for 28–35
Children's Museum of Manhattan
  32, 35
Chinatown *21*, 23, *43*, 49
Christmas 100–101
Chrysler Building *89*, 94, 99
churches
  Abyssinian Baptist Church *148*, 153
  The Cathedral Church of St. John
    the Divine *149*, 151
  St. Mark's Church in-the-Bowery
    61
  St. Patrick's Cathedral *18*, 22, *89*,
    93–94
  St. Paul's Chapel 47
  Trinity Church 23, *42*, 47–48
City Pass 9
climate 176
The Cloisters *148*, 154–155
comedy venues 65
Conservatory Garden *122*, 127

D

The Dakota *135*, 136–137
disabilities, travelers with 179
driving 177

E

East Village 57, *59*, 60–61
Ed Koch Queensboro Bridge 171
El Museo del Barrio *149*, 150
Ellis Island *42*, 44, 50–51
emergencies 179
Empire State Building *14*, 16, *19*, 22,
    24, 26, *73*, 78, 99
ethnic groups 52–53
events & festivals 176–177

F

FAO Schwarz *33*, 34
fashion 82–83
Federal Hall National Memorial
  43, 47
Federal Reserve Bank of New
  York 46
Fifth Avenue *14*, 16, *24*, 26
Flatiron Building *72*, 75–76
Fraunces Tavern *42*, 45–46
free attractions 9
Frick Collection *105*, 106

G

galleries 116–117
Gateway National Recreation
  Area 172
General Grant National Memorial
  149, 151
Gracie Mansion 111
Gramercy Park *73*, 76–77
Grand Central Terminal *89*, 94
Greenwich Village *20*, 23, *25*, 27, 55,
    57, *59*, 64–65, 68

H

Halloween Parade 65
Hans Christian Andersen Statue 17
Harlem 53, 69
  see also The Heights & Harlem
Harlem Renaissance 156–157
Hayden Planetarium 141
The Heights & Harlem *38*, 146–157,
    148–149
  Abyssinian Baptist Church *148*, 153
  Apollo Theater *149*, 152
  Cathedral Church of St. John the
    Divine *149*, 151
  The Cloisters *148*, 154–155
  El Museo del Barrio *149*, 150
  General Grant National Memorial
    149, 151
  hotels 187
  Morris-Jumel Mansion *148*, 153
  The Studio Museum in Harlem
    149, 152
The High Line *20*, 23, *25*, 27, *58*, 63
Hotel Chelsea *72*, 74–75, 182
hotels 180–187

I

ice skating 100–101

immigrants 50, 51, 52–53
Intrepid Sea, Air & Space Museum
  88, 90
Italian American Museum 53

J
jazz 68–69, 137, 157
Jewish Museum 104, 109

K
kayaking 130–131
Koreatown 16

L
Lennon, John 126
Lincoln Center 135, 138–139
Liz Christy Bowery-Houston
  Garden 23
Loeb Boathouse 123, 125
Lower East Side 54, 128
The Lower East Side Tenement
  Museum 28, 30–31
Lower Manhattan 39, 40–51,
  42–43
  Battery Park 42, 44
  Chinatown 21, 23, 43, 49
  Ellis Island 42, 44, 50–51
  Federal Hall National Memorial
    43, 47
  Fraunces Tavern 43, 45–46
  hotels 180–181
  National Museum of the
    American Indian 42, 44–45
  South Street Seaport Historic
    District 43, 48–49
  Statue of Liberty National
    Monument 42, 44, 50–51
  Trinity Church 23, 42, 47–48
  Wall Street 21, 43, 46
  World Trade Center Site 21,
    42, 48

M
Madame Tussauds 88, 92
Madison Avenue 118–119
Madison Square Park 73, 77
The Mall 123, 124
markets 61, 62, 101, 144, 166
Meatpacking District 20, 55, 58,
  62–63
Merchant's House Museum 59, 61
Metropolitan Museum of Art 14, 17,
  105, 112–115

Metropolitan Opera House 138
Midtown North 39, 86–97, 88–89
  Chrysler Building 89, 94, 99
  Grand Central Terminal 89, 94
  hotels 183–185
  Intrepid Sea, Air & Space
    Museum 88, 90
  Madame Tussauds 88, 92
  Museum of Modern Art 18, 22,
    89, 96–97
  Rockefeller Center 14, 17, 19, 89,
    92–93, 99, 100
  St. Patrick's Cathedral 18, 22, 89,
    93–94
  Times Square 14, 17, 19, 88, 90–91
  United Nations Headquarters
    89, 95
Midtown South 39, 70–81, 72–73
  Empire State Building 15, 16, 19,
    22, 25, 26, 73, 78, 99
  Flatiron Building 72, 75–76
  Gramercy Park 73, 76–77
  Hotel Chelsea 72, 74–75
  hotels 182–183
  Madison Square Park 73, 77
  Morgan Library & Museum 73,
    78–79
  New York Public Library 73,
    79–81
  Rubin Museum of Art 72, 74
Morgan Library & Museum 73,
  78–79
Morris-Jumel Mansion 148, 153
movie locations 128–129
museum opening times 8
museums
  American Folk Art Museum 135,
    139
  American Museum of Natural
    History 32, 35, 134, 140–141
  Asia Society and Museum 53
  Brooklyn Museum 161, 168–169
  Children's Museum of Manhattan
    32, 35
  The Cloisters 148, 154–155
  El Museo del Barrio 149, 150
  Fraunces Tavern 43, 45–46
  Frick Collection 105, 106
  Intrepid Sea, Air & Space
    Museum 88, 90

Italian American Museum 53
Jewish Museum 104, 109
Lower East Side Tenement
  Museum 29, 30–31
Merchant's House Museum 59,
  61
Metropolitan Museum of Art 14,
  17, 105, 112–115
Morgan Library & Museum 73,
  78–79
Morris-Jumel Mansion 148, 153
Museum of American Finance 46
Museum of Chinese in America
  49
Museum of Modern Art 18, 22,
  89, 96–97
Museum of the City of New York
  104, 110
National Jazz Museum in Harlem
  157
National Museum of the
  American Indian 42, 44–45
New York City Fire Museum 29
New York City Police Museum
  29, 30
New-York Historical Society 135,
  136
Rubin Museum of Art 72, 74
Seaport Museum 29, 30, 48
Solomon R. Guggenheim
  Museum 104, 107–109
The Studio Museum in Harlem
  149, 152
Whitney Museum of American
  Art 105, 106–107
music 22, 47–48, 60–61, 65,
  68–69, 77, 137, 138, 153,
  157, 166

N
National Arts Club 76
National Jazz Museum in Harlem
  157
National Museum of the American
  Indian 42, 44–45
NBC Studios 24, 26
The New York Botanical Garden 172
New York City Fire Museum 29, 31
The New York City Police Museum
  29, 30
New York Public Library 73, 79–81

INDEX

New-York Historical Society *135*, 136
Nolita 54–55

O

observation decks 34, 51, 93
one-day tours 14–17, 24–27
orientation 177
outdoor activities 130–131

P

Paley Park 16
Park Slope *160*, 166–167
parks & gardens 172–173
    Battery Park *42*, 44
    Brooklyn Botanic Garden *161*,
        164–165, 172
    Bryant Park 81, 101
    Carl Schurz Park *105*, 110–111
    Central Park see Central Park
    Gateway National Recreation
        Area 172
    Gramercy Park *73*, 76–77
    The High Line *20*, 23, *25*, 27,
        58, 63
    Liz Christy Bowery-Houston
        Garden 23
    Madison Square Park *73*, 77
    New York Botanical Garden 172
    Pelham Bay Park 173
    Prospect Park *161*, 166, 172
    Riverside Park *134*, 139
    Staten Island Greenbelt 173
    Union Square Park *20*, *59*, 62
    Pelham Bay Park 173
    Prospect Park *161*, 166
public transportation 177–179

R

Radio City Music Hall 93, 99
The Ramble 17
Riverside Park *134*, 139
Rockefeller Center *14*, 17, *18*, 89,
    92–93, 99, 100
Rubin Museum of Art *72*, 74
running 130

S

safety 179
St. Mark's Church in-the-Bowery 61
St. Patrick's Cathedral *18*, 22, 89,
    93–94
St. Paul's Chapel 47
The Scholastic Store *28*, 31

Seaport Museum *29*, 30, 48
seasons 176
Shakespeare Garden *122*, 127
shopping
    Downtown 54–55
    fashion shopping 83
    Fifth Avenue 26
    gourmet food shops 144–145
    museum shops 119
    Upper East Side 118–119
SoHo *15*, 17, 54
Solomon R. Guggenheim Museum
    104, 107–109
Sony Wonder Technology Lab
    33, 34
South Street Seaport Historic
    District *43*, 48–49
The Standard *25*, 27, 85, 182
Staten Island Ferry *21*, 23
Staten Island Greenbelt 173
Statue of Liberty National
    Monument *42*, 44, 50–51
Stonewall Inn 65
Strawberry Fields *123*, 126
street food 17
The Studio Museum in Harlem
    149, 152
subways 178
swimming 131

T

taxis 178–179
theater 9, 65
Theodore Roosevelt Birthplace 77
Tiffany & Co. *24*, 26
Time Warner Center *135*, 137
Times Square *15*, 17, *19*, 88, 90–91
Top of the Rock *33*, 34, 93
Trinity Church 23, *43*, 47–48
Trump Tower 16
TV tours 129

U

Union Square Park *20*, *59*, 62
United Nations Headquarters 89, 95
Upper East Side *39*, 102–119,
    104–105
    Carl Schurz Park *105*, 110–111
    Frick Collection *105*, 106
    hotels 185–186
    Jewish Museum *104*, 109

Metropolitan Museum of Art *14*,
    17, *105*, 112–115
Museum of the City of New York
    104, 110
Solomon R. Guggenheim
    Museum *104*, 107–109
Whitney Museum of American
    Art *105*, 106–107
Upper West Side *38*, 132–143,
    134–135
    American Folk Art Museum *135*,
        139
    American Museum of Natural
        History *32*, 35, *134*, 140–141
    The Dakota *135*, 136–137
    hotels 186–187
    Lincoln Center *135*, 138–139
    New-York Historical Society *135*,
        136
    Riverside Park *134*, 139
    Time Warner Center *135*, 137

V

Verrazano-Narrows Bridge 171
Vesuvio Playground 17
The Villages *39*, 56–65, *58–59*
    East Village 57, *59*, 60–61
    Greenwich Village *20*, 23, *25*, 27,
        55, 57, *58*, 64–65, 68
    The High Line *20*, 23, *25*, 27, *58*,
        63
    hotels 181–182
    Meatpacking District *20*, 55, *58*,
        62–63
    Merchant's House Museum *59*,
        61
    Union Square Park *20*, *59*, 62
visitor information 176

W

Wall Street *21*, *43*, 46
Washington Square Arch 65
websites 177
weekend tours 18–23, 28–35
Whitney Museum of American Art
    105, 106–107
World Trade Center Site *21*, *43*, 48
writers 65, 66–67, 156–157

Z

zoos *33*, 35, *123*, 124, 166

CREDITS

Authors

Katherine Cancila

Additional text by Lisa Armstrong, Eleanor Berman, Christina Cush, Margie Goldsmith, Diana Greenwald, Randy Hecht, Rob Kimmel, Judy Kirkwood, Marni Kleinfield-Hayes, Chris Michel, Linda Tagliaferro, Sarah Wolf, Joe Yogerst, Cristi Young

Picture Credits

t = top; b = bottom, l = left; r = right, m = middle

2-3 Alex Segre/Alamy. 4 Amanda Hall/Robert Harding Travel/www.photolibrary.com. 5tr Michelle Bennett/Lonely Planet Images. 5bl Courtesy of Jeanne M.Beaumon/Museum of the City of New York/MCNY02/The Art Archive. 5mr Alan Gallery/Alamy. 6 Jean-Pierre Lescourret/Imagebroker.net/www.photolibrary.com. 9 Wayne Fodgen/Ticket/www.photolibrary.com. 12-13 Ilja Mašík/Shutterstock. 14l Ramin Talaie/Corbis. 14r Bildagenturm/Tips Italia/www.photolibrary.com. 15 Frances M.Roberts/Alamy. 16 Michael S.Yamashita/Corbis. 18r Radius Images/www.photolibrary.com. 18l Sam Chadwick/Shutterstock. 19l Songquan Deng/Dreamstime.com. 19r Cedric Weber/Shutterstock. 20 Richard Levine/Alamy. 21l Tony Savino/Corbis. 21r fotog/Tetra Images/www.photolibrary.com. 22 Bertrand Gardel/Hemis/www.photolibrary.com. 24l Natalija Sirokova/Shutterstock. 24r Stock Connection Blue/Alamy. 25tl Dimitrios Kambouris/Getty Images. 25tr Supri Shuharjoto/Shutterstock. 25b Andria Patino/Age fotostock/www.photolibrary.com. 26 Len Holsborg/Alamy. 28l Scholastic. 28tr Ramin Talaie/Corbis. 29l New York City Fire Museum. 29r Sepavo/Dreamstime.com. 31 Scholastic. 32l Copyright of www.johnabbottphoto.com. 32r Mark & Audrey Gibson/www.photolibrary.com. 33, 34 Sony Wonder Technology Lab. 36-37 Giuseppe Masci/Tips Italia/www.photolibrary.com. 40 Cameron Davidson/Corbis. 42m The National Museum of the American Indian. 42b Caitlin Mirra/Shutterstock. 43 dbimages/Alamy. 45 Photo Equipe 153/Cuboimages/www.photolibrary.com. 47 Ben Pipe/Ticket/www.photolibrary.com. 49 sevapo/Shutterstock. 50 Library of Congress. 52 Keiko Niwa, courtesy Lower East Side Tenement Museum. 53 Michael S.Yamashita/Corbis. 55 Dan Herrick/Lonely Planet Images. 56 Walter Weissman/Corbis. 58tl Peter Bennett/Ambient Images/www.photolibrary.com. 58bl James Leynse/Corbis. 59t AA World Travel Library/Alamy. 59mr Merchant's House Museum. 60 Dan Herrick/Lonely Planet Images. 63 Alex Segre/Alamy. 64 Eye Ubiquitous/www.photolibrary.com. 66 Allen Ginsberg/Corbis. 67 Neville Elder/Corbis. 69 Larry Busacca/Getty Images. 70 Hermann Dobler/Imagebroker.net/www.photolibrary.com. 72tl Rubin Museum of Art, C2006.41.1 (HAR 65692. 72bl Songquan Deng/Shutterstock. 73tr Rafael Macia/Ticket/www.photolibrary.com. 73br Jim Zuckerman/Flirt Collection/www.photolibrary.com. 75 Barry Winiker/Ticket/www.photolibrary.com. 76 Richard Cummins/Robert Harding Travel/www.photolibrary.com. 79 Vittorio Sciosia/Cuboimages/www.photolibrary.com. 80 Gavin Hellier/Robert Harding Travel/www.photolibrary.com. 82 Jutta Klee/FStop/www.photolibrary.com. 83 Ludovic Maisant/Hemis/www.photolibrary.com. 85 Jin Lee/Bloomberg/Getty Images. 86 Andrew F.Kazmierski/Shutterstock. 88t Jorg Hackemann/Shutterstock. 88b Timothy A.Clary/AFP/Getty Images. 89 Marcin Wasilewski/Shutterstock. 91 Andrey Bayda/Shutterstock. 92 Songquan Deng/Shutterstock. 95 Tetra Images/www.photolibrary.com. 96 Kordcom/Age fotostock/www.photolibrary.com. 98 Ambient Images Inc./Superstock. 99 Mishella/Shutterstock. 101 Richard Green/Alamy. 102 Michelle Bennett/Lonely Planet Images. 104tr Courtesy of Jeanne M.Beaumon/Museum of the City of New York/MCNY02/The Art Archive. 104bl Christian Kober/Robert Harding Travel/www.photolibrary.com. 104tl Jeff Greenberg/www.photolibrary.com. 105r Rudi Von Briel/www.photolibrary.com. 105l Tom Pepeira/Iconotec/www.photolibrary.com. 106 Bryan Bedder/Getty Images. 108 Christian Kober/Robert Harding Travel/www.photolibrary.com. 111 Peter Bennett/Ambient Images/www.photolibrary.com. 112 Herman Dobler/Imagebroker.net/www.photolibrary.com. 114 Barry Winiker/Ticket/www.photolibrary.com. 116 Mama Bear by Tom Otterness, On view at Marlborough Gallery, booth 402, Pier 92/Image credit: David Willems, Courtesy of The Armory Show. 117 Illumination (2008), Installation by Ai WeiWei © Ai WeiWei/Photo Courtesy of Mary Boone Gallery, New York. 119 Ingolf Pompe/LOOK-foto/www.photolibrary.com. 120 Jean-Pierre Lescourret/Superstock/www.photolibrary.com. 122m John A.Anderson/Shutterstock. 122b Richard A.McGuirk/Shutterstock. 123mr redswept/Shutterstock. 123bm Gail Mooney/Corbis. 125 Andria Patino/Corbis. 127 Sandra Baker/Alamy. 128 Spencer Grant/Alamy. 129 Paramount/The Kobal Collection. 131 Demetrio Carrasco/JAI/Corbis. 132 Frances Roberts/Alamy. 134r Francesco Tomasinelli/Tips Italia/www.photolibrary.com. 134l Jeff Greenberg/Age fotostock/www.photolibrary.com. 135tl © Collection of the New-York Historical Society, USA/The Bridgeman Art Library. 135br Mike Liu/Shutterstock. 135bl Barry Winiker/Ticket/www.photolibrary.com. 136 © Collection of the New-York Historical Society, USA/The Bridgeman Art Library. 138 sevapo/Shutterstock.com. 140 Renaud Visage/Age fotostock/www.photolibrary.com. 142 Gregory James Van Raalte/Shutterstock. 143 Colin D.Young/Shutterstock. 145 Andrew Pini/Fresh Food Images/www.photolibrary.com. 146 Barry Winiker/www.photolibrary.com. 148 Morris-Jumel Mansion. 149tl Thos Robinson/Getty Images. 149bl Dave Bowman/Alamy. 149br P.Deliss/Godong/Corbis. 150 La Cama (The Bed), 1987 by Pepón Osorio, Mixed Media Installation, Collection El Museo del Barrio, New York. 152 Peter Bennett/Ambient Images/www.photolibrary.com. 154 William Manning/Alamy. 156 Courtesy, The Lilly Library, Indiana University, Bloomington, Indiana. 157 Frank Driggs Collection/Getty Images. 158 Bill Wassman/Lonely Planet Images. 160t SVLuma/Shutterstock. 160b Alan Gallery/Alamy. 161t Brooklyn Museum. 161br Rick Shupper/Ambient Images/www.photolibrary.com. 163 Mark Peterson/Corbis. 164 Jackie Weisberg/Ambient Images/www.photolibrary. 167 Thistle Hill Tavern. 168 Brooklyn Museum. 170 Tobbe/Corbis. 171 Ron Chapple Stock/www.photolibrary.com. 173 Vladimir Korostyshevskiy/Shutterstock. 174-175 Allan Baxter/Photodisc/Getty Images.

Front cover David Joyner/istockphoto; Nikada/iStockphoto

Walking New York

Published by the National Geographic Society

John M. Fahey, Jr., *Chairman of the Board and Chief Executive Officer*
Timothy T. Kelly, *President*
Declan Moore, *Executive Vice President; President, Publishing*
Melina Gerosa Bellows, *Executive Vice President, Chief Creative Officer, Books, Kids, and Family*

Prepared by the Book Division

Barbara Brownell Grogan, *Vice President and Editor in Chief*
Jonathan Halling, *Design Director, Books and Children's Publishing*
Marianne R. Koszorus, *Design Director, Books*
Barbara A. Noe, *Senior Editor*
Carl Mehler, *Director of Maps*
Marty Ittner, *Design Consultant*
Leslie Allen, Lise Sajewski, Anne Smyth, *Contributors*
R. Gary Colbert, *Production Director*
Mike Horenstein, *Production Manager*
Jennifer A. Thornton, *Managing Editor*
Meredith C. Wilcox, *Administrative Director, Illustrations*

Travel Publications

Keith Bellows, *Vice President and Editor-in-Chief*
Jerry Sealy, *Director of Design*

Manufacturing and Quality Management

Christopher A. Liedel, *Chief Fi*
Phillip L. Schlosser, *Senior Vice*
Chris Brown, *Technical Directo*
Nicole Elliott, *Manager*
Rachel Faulise, *Manager*
Robert L. Barr, *Manager*

Created by Toucan Books

Ellen Dupont, *Editorial Directc*
Alice Peebles, *Senior Editor*
Pete Clubb, Jane Hutchings, *Anna Southgate, Editors*
Leah Germann, *Designer*
Christine Vincent, *Picture Mai*
Sharon Southren, *Picture Rese*
Merritt Cartographic, *Maps*
Beth Landis Hester, *Proofread*
Marie Lorimer, *Indexer*

CREDITS